Tomslake
History of the Sudeten Germans in Canada

Andrew Amstatter

Copyright © 1978 ANDREW AMSTATTER
ISBN 0-88839-002-5

Amstatter, Andrew.
  Tomslake

  Bibliography: p.
  Includes index.
  ISBN 0-88839-002-5

  1. Germans in British Columbia—History.
  2. Germans in Czechoslovakia—History.
  I. Title.
  FC3850.G3A47   971.1'004'31   C78-002093-6
  F1089.7.G3A47

Funding assistance by the Multiculturalism Directorate, Department of the Secretary of State, is gratefully acknowledged.

Published simultaneously in Canada and the United States by:

HANCOCK HOUSE PUBLISHERS LTD.
3215 Island View Road   SAANICHTON, B.C. V0S 1M0

HANCOCK HOUSE PUBLISHERS INC.
12008 1st Avenue South   SEATTLE, WA. 98168

TABLE OF CONTENTS

    Dedication 4
    Acknowledgement 5
    Foreword 6
    Introduction 8
    Preface 19
1 Germans in Czechoslovakia 21
2 Becoming Political Refugees 33
3 With the Help of Friends 45
4 Flight to Freedom and Exile 59
5 Emigration 67
6 Fears and First Impressions 73
7 The Land Settlement Company 83
8 The First Year 89
9 Frustration and Humiliation 99
10 Our Own Farms 107
11 Hazards 115
12 A Community Develops 121
13 Language and Education 129
14 Women and Work 137
15 Time Out From Work 143
16 Visitors and Neighbors 149
17 Changes Through Time 155
18 The Alpha and Omega 163
    Appendix I Financial Statements and Map . . 169
    Appendix II Male Settlers at Tupper Creek, 1939 . 179
    Notes on Sources 181
    Suggested Reading List 181

DEDICATION

This book is dedicated to the memory of those who lost their lives during the struggle for freedom in our native land, or suffered imprisonment during the Nazi regime, and to my mother. Eva Amstatter suffered the anguish of having two sons imprisoned in Dachau. She never knew whether a third son, myself, succeeded in escaping to freedom.

ACKNOWLEDGEMENT

I wish to acknowledge with sincere thanks the many individuals and institutions whose help has enabled me to write a more comprehensive story than would otherwise have been possible. The Seliger Archive in Stuttgart, Germany, gave me permission to use data from their book **Menschen im Exil**, foremost of which are the British Press reports. Notes made by the late Valentin Dittrich on the earliest days of the Tomslake settlement were of great value. So was the material I received from the late Willi Schoen of Dawson Creek, B.C. and Mr. Henry Weisbach, Toronto, Ontario, both of whom were settlers and group leaders from the start of the settlement. Also helpful were Mr. Alois Mollik, Pouce Coupe, B.C., and Mr. Ernst Paul, Esslingen, Germany, who corroborated some facts for me. Thanks also to Mr. Weir of the Northern Alberta Dairy Pool in Dawson Creek, B.C., for providing recent information on the dairy industry of the area.

Last but not least I thank my wife, Mary Ann and our three daughters, Eileen, Janice, and Evelyn, for their encouragement while writing. Special thanks to Mary Ann for her patience.

Andrew Amstatter

FOREWORD

For hundreds of years Sudeten Germans inhabited the border areas of Bohemia, Moravia and Silesia. They lived under various regimes. In more recent history, they were citizens of Austria-Hungry but, in 1918, without their consultation, became citizens of the newly formed state of Czechoslovakia. Three times in the last sixty years Sudeten Germans became objects of world politics, in 1918, in 1938 and in 1945, each time without having a chance to decide their own fate.

From 1918 until 1938 they lived under the regime of Czechoslovakia. Hitler's reign of terror began in Germany in 1933. Austria was swallowed up not long after and the Sudeten Germans in Czechoslovakia realized they were next.

The democratic sector of the Sudeten Germans fought up to the last minute to save a state which during its existence had done them no particular favors. However, they believed it would be better to live in relative freedom than subject to Hitler's terror.

Their efforts were to no avail. England, France, Italy and Germany decided at the Munich Conference on September 30th, 1938, that the Sudeten areas of Czechoslovakia were to be handed over to Germany by October 1st, 1938. Again, the Sudeten Germans were not asked for their opinion. The result was thousands of Sudeten German Social Democrats who stood up against the Nazis had to flee into exile, while other thousands ended up in concentration camps.

Through the efforts of the leadership of the Social Democratic Party, more than 1,000 Sudeten Refugees were admitted to Canada in the summer of 1939 to be settled as farmers by the CPR and CNR Colonization Departments. Half the refugees were settled in the Peace River District of British Columbia, while the other half were settled in Northern Saskatchewan.

The author of TOMSLAKE attempts to do two things. First he attempts to familiarize the reader with the background of the Sudeten German refugees who came to Canada in 1939 and secondly he attempts to picture the life and experiences of these refugees as pioneers in Northern British Columbia. When one realizes that most of them had not been farmers in their homeland, it should be evident that there was a tremendous task involved in their learning the Canadian way of life, the Canadian way of farming and in dealing with the many hazards involved. The author, personally acquainted as he is with the many happenings in the settlement, pictures the transition of factory and office workers to Canadian farmers. He creates a story of the settlement which should be known to Canadians everywhere.

One does not have to agree with all the conclusions of Mr. Amstatter, but it must be admitted that he has done a vast amount of work to produce his account of life in the settlement.

This book would not have been possible without the help the author received from many persons in the settlement. In particular, it would not have been possible without an editing and publication grant made available to the Central Organization of Sudeten German Clubs in Canada by the Multicultural Program, Government of Canada.

May TOMSLAKE help to bring about a better understanding of the tremendous work these Sudeten German settlers did in Northern British Columbia.

Henry Weisbach, President
Central Organization of Sudeten-German Clubs in Canada

INTRODUCTION

Andrew Amstatter's **TOMSLAKE** is the first attempt by a Sudeten German Canadian to record and publish his pioneer reminiscences, and as such it has historical value, both in terms of the European background to World War II and the settling of the Canadian West. Amstatter was in the Sudetenland experiencing Nazi terror at a time when Canadians were still largely ignorant of Adolf Hitler's plans to conquer the world, but unlike so many other Europeans he was able to escape the holocaust of 1939-1945. But his distaste for fascism spurred him to join the Canadian Army and to spend one year in Europe, and like so many Canadians during World War II he played a part in destroying the Nazi regime. His personal experiences in the Sudetenland are the very stuff of history, though far too often historians are concerned only with the major personalities and the events which take place in chancellories, embassies, and the conference halls. Amstatter's personal reminiscences, on the other hand, are European history from the point of view of the man in the street. The same may be said of his pioneering experiences in Canada. His account of the settlement of Tomslake is different from the impressions one would form after a visit of the Public Archives of Canada or the Glenbow Alberta Archives, the depository for the Canadian Pacific Railway's Canada Colonization Association Papers. There one finds only the official view of what it was like to settle some 500 people at Tomslake; the logistics of providing food, shelter, implements, and clearing land. Amstatter, on the other hand, recounts in a very personal way the frustrations experienced by the Sudetens in dealing with certain CPR officials, the weather, machinery, livestock, and in carving farms out of the bush. He also gives credit where it is due and highlights the role of women and the manner in which they adjusted to and contributed to life in an area which, prior to the arrival of the Sudetens, was only lightly settled by English-speaking Canadians.

The special nature of the Tomslake settlement sets it apart from earlier immigration efforts by the CPR, but life on a homestead in the Peace River block in the period 1939-1942 was much the same as it had been in other parts of the West in years past. The weather had always been a problem and machinery had always broken down; water had frequently been bad and the soil of an indifferent quality; and the settler unable to speak English. None of the problems encountered by the Sudetens were new, but the pioneer reminiscences of Andrew Amstatter bring them into focus and illustrate what it was like to homestead in northeastern British Columbia during World War II. Therein lies the real value of TOMSLAKE:

Bonar A. Gow, Ph.D.
Northern Lights College
Dawson Creek, B.C.

GERMAN AREAS OF SETTLEMENT WITHIN BOHEMIA AND MORAVIA-SILESIA

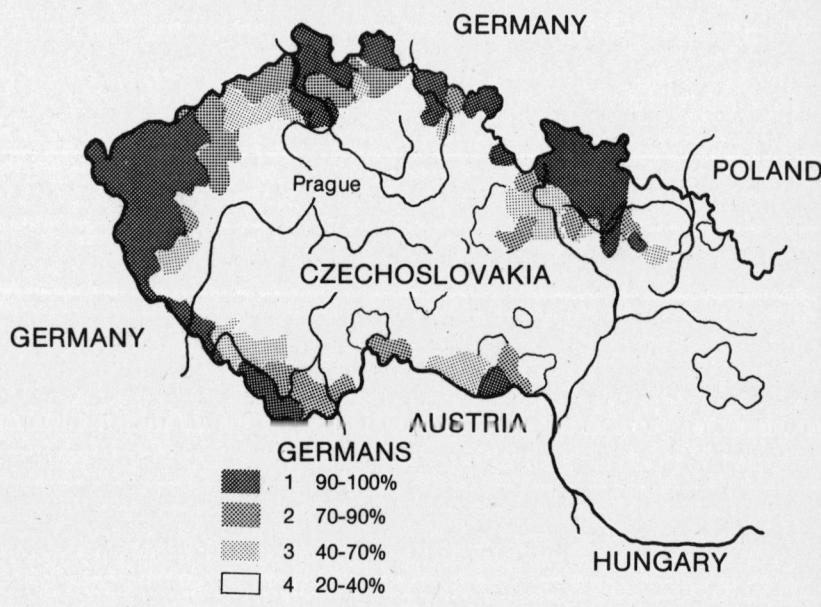

The map is based on census of 1930. J. Chmelar, Le probleme allemand en Tchecoslovaquie.

TERRITORIES SEPARATED FROM THE CZECHOSLOVAK REPUBLIC AFTER THE PACT OF MUNICH IN 1938

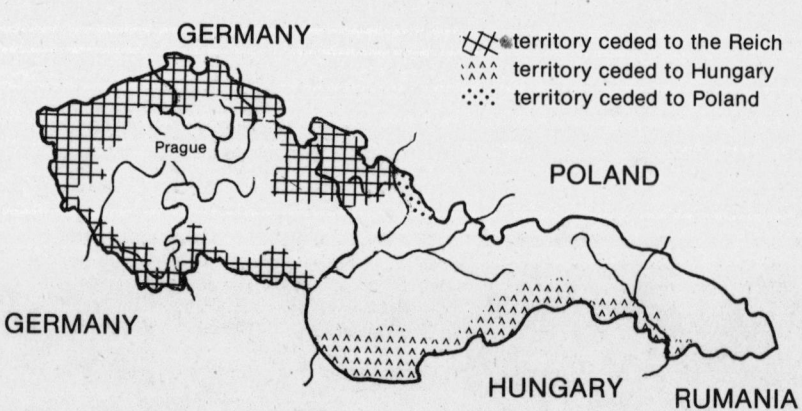

German-Czechoslovak border of November 20, 1938.

A group of Sudeten German Anti-Nazis in Grasslitz were marched in October 1938 to a prison to be transfered to Dachau concentration camp.

Wald-Kraiburg. Bunkers like the one above became temporary housing for thousands of homeless people after the earth and trees serving as camouflage had been removed from the top.

Plochingen-Stumphof. A row of new apartment buildings. Construction is still going on strong.

Plochingen. This picture is an air photograph of this part of Plochingen at the present.

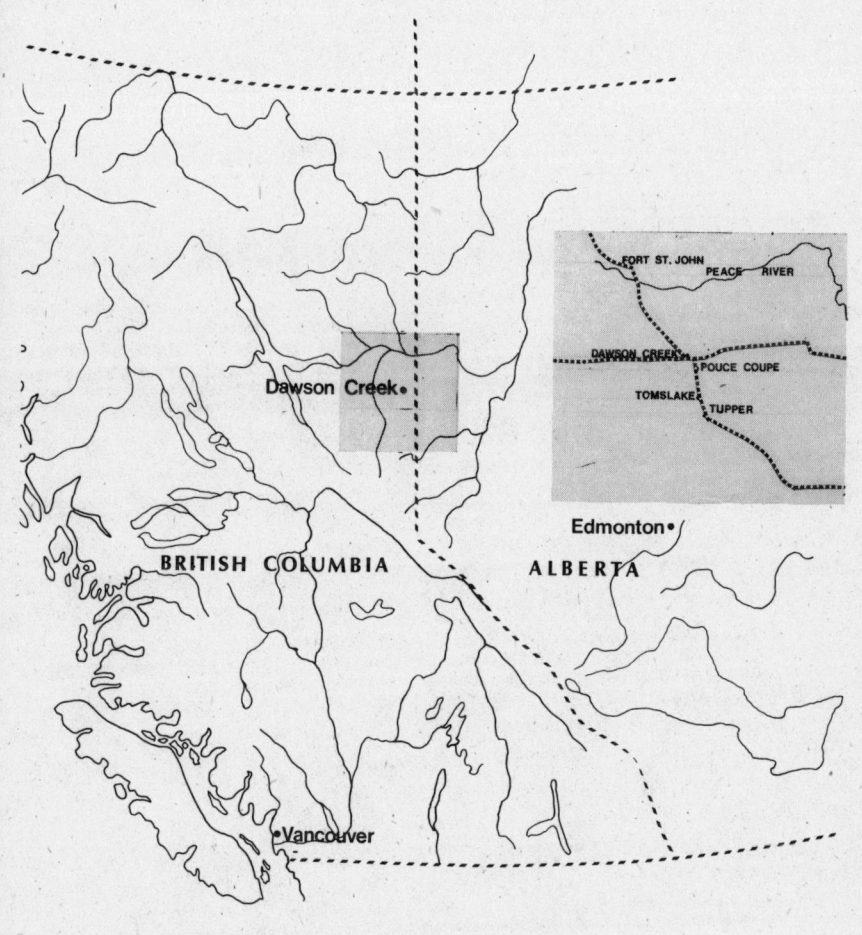

Settler family at Tupper Station with all their earthly goods.

Hauling water from Tupper Creek.

This old dilapitated blacksmith shop became not only the center of all repair work on the machinery, but also a place for settler meetings.

The women of the settlers carried a heavy load and deserve credit for the success of the settlement.

The Sudeten Settlement started out with seven groups of frame shacks like the ones in this picture. These shacks were 18 feet long and 14 feet wide and all the crowded living in it had to go on for many years, before better housing could be afforded by the settlers.
After all the prospective settlers had arrived by August 1939, a meeting was held to discuss settlement problems.

PREFACE

The story of the Sudeten Germans, contained in these chapters, is neither a personal story nor a complete account of their experiences. My intention in writing this book was to record a sample of the experiences we shared and to describe to Canadian readers, under forty-five years of age, some events about which they may know little.

The Sudeten Germans, who came to Canada just before World War II, came as political refugees. Two groups were settled in western Canada; one, on farms near St. Walburg in northern Saskatchewan; the other, in bushland in the Peace River area of British Columbia. I was a member of the group settled in British Columbia. My experiences during escape, exile, and resettlement are not unique, but a sample of those experienced by several hundred others. The trials we shared are a tribute to those now resting in the ground which we transformed from wilderness to civilization, and to those senior citizens who are looking on as their children and grandchildren carry on the work they began.

After a few pages of the story had been written I realized that many readers would not understand the reasons for our flight from Czechoslovakia. The events described in chapters one and two are the background to our status as political refugees. I have included this background in the belief that historic events can become a good teacher, if following generations read about them and draw conclusions from them for the good of their future.

This story deals with facts, either as the writer experienced them or learned about them from others. All the names mentioned are those of real people. Some individuals are identified by initials only, to avoid embarrassment to them and their relatives.

Material from German sources has been translated by me. The quotations from British press reports, for example, may not exactly correspond with the original text. Nevertheless, the meaning is accurately conveyed.

If readers who learned English in school find flaws in my composition or grammar I beg your forgiveness. I was never fortunate enough to have had the opportunity to attend English classes. After twenty years as a pioneer farmer I moved to the city, where the struggle to survive by hard physical labor prevented an aging man from attending evening courses. What English I have learned, I learned while serving in the Canadian forces during World War II.

1

GERMANS IN CZECHOSLOVAKIA

The state of Czechoslovakia as it appears today on the map of Europe is the result of agreements made following two world wars. The territory occupied by Czechoslovakia has a long history of different ethnic groups living together. Two groups have dominated the territory: the Slavs and the Germans. People of both cultures entered the area many centuries ago and prospered from the rich agricultural land, the deposits of copper, silver and coal in the mountains, and the trade which developed between eastern and western Europe. Conflicts among feudal rulers over territorial control and religious beliefs scarred the area and its people prior to the sixteenth century. With the death of the King of Bohemia and Hungary, in 1526, the area became part of the Austro-Hungarian empire. Czechoslovakia was then the principalities of Bohemia and Moravia.

Under the Hapsburgs, the German language and culture tended to dominate the area. Early in the seventeenth century Czech noblemen resisted this domination. The Thirty Years War began as a result of resistance to an intolerant Hapsburg king. One of the early battles of this war saw the defeat of the Czech nobility. The Czech population was left without leadership, as the majority of the Czech upper class migrated. Czech culture became the culture of the peasants and working men. Despite official recognition of both the Czech and German languages, from the seventeenth century onward, the population was divided by economic and language differences. The upper strata were German: the lower strata were Czech.

Eighteenth century Hapsburg rulers were interested in

economic development and education within the empire. In particular, Empress Maria Theresa and her son, and successor, Joseph II, worked to improve the conditions of their subjects. Administrative reform, to speed up and simplify the administration of various principalities, brought about the unification of the two principalities and Austria. To ensure that imperial regulations were understood by the poorer people of the area, administrators assigned to the region were required to have some knowledge of the Czech language. During the same period, public education began. German was the language of instruction throughout the empire. By royal decree, in 1784, German became the only official language of the Austro-Hungarian empire.

Royal interest in economic development encouraged immigration, into Bohemia and Moravia, by those willing to invest capital. German investors were attracted to areas where German textile manufacturers had established factories earlier in the century. Immigration strengthened the German influence in the economy. The migration of the Czech nobility in the previous century had resulted in many Germans becoming the owners of agricultural land. Feudal land holding prevailed and the Czech peasant was a serf. Concern by the royal household for the plight of the peasant brought about the decision to encourage voluntary regulation of the terms of service. Proclamation of religious freedom and relaxation of censorship, during the last quarter of the eighteenth century, provided greater freedom for all subjects of the empire.

The final decade of the eighteenth century and the first half of the nineteenth century brought significant changes in the status of the Czech language and culture in Bohemia and Moravia. A new ruler, Leopold II, reversed many of his predecessor's decisions regarding official languages and administrative divisions in the Empire. He requested that his subjects present their grievances directly to him for solution. Leopold informally recognized the Czech culture by attending Czech theatrical performances and indicating his willingness to consider education in the Czech language. The spirit of nationalism, which emerged during this period in Europe, sparked a revival of interest in little known cultures. German writers, aristocrats, and Bohemian Germans became interested in the Slavic culture. The peace and social equality of Czech culture was a favorable contrast to the social inequality and conflict of prominent European cultures at the time. Within Bohemia and Moravia the local aristocracy, firmly opposed to the absolute rule of the imperial dynasty, encouraged provincial control of local administration. To strengthen their position they took up the Czech language. The combination of aristocratic, cultural, and political interests resulted in an awakening of Czech consciousness to their ethnic heritage.

In general, the aristocracy was unsympathetic to revolutionary ideas of racial or ethnic nations. Instead, the Austro-Hungarian rulers attempted to create territorial allegiance. Bohemian and Moravian patriotism was encouraged in the hope that it would replace both German and Slav notions of nationalism.

Slav and German nationalism was narrowly based on language and racial unity rather than territorial unity and equality. Nationalism strengthened as industrialization created a working class, and peasant discontent forced land reform. The economic development of Bohemia expanded with the development of transcontinental trade. By mid-1800, Bohemia became the industrial heartland of the Austro-Hungarian empire with its coal mines, ironworks, textile mills and skeleton railway system. Emancipation of the peasants, in 1848, benefited the better-off peasants, who became independent land owners. At the same time poorer peasants unable to obtain land and no longer protected from starvation by feudal lords, left the land for work in industry. When news of the French workers revolt of 1848 reached Bohemia and Moravia, it reinforced the desire for democratic rather than autocratic rule. The Imperial government agreed to introduce democratic principles into the administration of its principalities. In Bohemia and Moravia, the question of which majority should rule became a serious problem. At first both Czechs and Germans advocated democracy without concern for the composition of the majority to rule. Earlier land reform had, however, tipped the balance toward a Czech majority. The imperial government rejected a constitutional proposal which would have divided the Czechs and Germans into ethnic settlements. Local government and a limited form of representative government would have intensified ethnic divisions. Instead, the Imperial government vaguely acknowledged the rights of ethnic groups and followed a confused policy toward cultural questions. Frustration of their aspirations lead the Czechs to conclude that the German government and its administration were their enemies.

A new constitution, enacted in 1867, contained a clause recognizing the equality of nationalities and languages of provinces in local administration and education. The politicians, pleased with their own generosity, failed to carry this legislation to practical application. A dual system of primary education eventually evolved in which children were educated in their local language. Secondary education was taught only in German. The economic aspirations of the growing Czech middle-class were frustrated by the lack of secondary education. Without adequate education the Czechs remained minor government officials, skilled tradesmen, and unskilled labor within an economic system owned or managed by Germans. The conflict over the language of education spread as expansion of industry in Bohemia in the eighteen sixties and seventies attracted the growing Czech population. The predominantly German population objected to the introduction of public and private Czech schools.

During the same period, Czech nationalist organizations promoted Czech industrial and cultural development. A Czech national bank, founded in 1868, financed industrial expansion under Czech ownership. These organizations also financed theaters and the division of the University of Prague into Czech and German institutions.

German nationalist organizations were formed for similar purposes. Radical groups openly condemned the Hapsburg empire for the tolerance of minority cultures, while others rejected the ideas of cultural or racial superiority. Impatient radical youths, both Czech and German, consistently disrupted any negotiations seeking a compromise between the two cultures to preserve peace in Bohemia and Moravia. The last decade of the nineteenth century saw civil war narrowly avoided as a result of the continuing conflict over the language of the courts, the administration, and the school system.

With increasing frequency following 1880, the Austro-

Hungarian monarchy chose to rule with the Czech majority. This enhanced their status within the empire and encouraged Czech interest in foreign affairs. Foreign policy and diplomacy had a direct bearing on Czech nationalist aspirations and they turned to France as their link with western European democracy. The internal divisions between Czechs and Germans were outwardly expressed by the pro-Slav, anti-German friendships established by the Czechs with other European countries. Similarly, the Germans made friends with anti-Slav, pro-German groups within the empire. By 1900, the Czechs and Germans of the Austro-Hungarian empire were separated not only by ethnic heritage but by associations with traditional antagonists.

Political passions cooled early in the twentieth century, making reform within the provinces possible. The Russian Revolution of 1905 stimulated Czech pride in Slavonic achievements and increased the activities of German democrats. Two important reforms resulted from the emotional exhaustion of the two sides and from the stimulation of labor politics. The Moravian Compromise of 1905 fixed the proportions of Czech and German representation in the provincial governments, set a minimum percentage for minorities to legally claim government services in their own language, and provided for local decisions regarding the language or languages of official use. Universal male suffrage was introduced in 1907. Representatives to the central parliament were elected in a ration of two Germans to one Czech to ensure adequate representation for the ten million Germans and six million Czechs in the provinces. National frontiers within Bohemia and Moravia remained as an attempt was made to maintain national unity within constituencies. This was impossible in constituencies of mixed population and local elections became nationalist competitions. Municipal governments continued to be elected by taxpayers only; therefore, control of local affairs remained in the hands of the rich. Even though Czech wealth had increased substantially, the Germans were more wealthy, particularly in industrialized Bohemia. Frustration of the Czech working man continued, as he could express his opinion on matters concerning the empire by voting in elections but was denied an opinion regarding local matters, such as the education of his children.

Narrowly defined nationalism continued to create and maintain Czech and German bitterness within the Austro-Hungarian empire. Neither group could resist chauvinism. Power in the society was in German hands while the increasing Czech population remained frustrated. Nationalistic rivalry dominated everyday life. National identity became a major consideration in hiring and firing of workers, and in the purchase of goods and services. The age old rivalry was not overcome by economic, political, and social change. The problem of ethnic origin was carried forward into the politics of a new country, Czechoslovakia.

The Austro-Hungarian Empire collapsed following World War 1 and several independent states were formed from its former principalities. The principle of self-determination and desire by western European nations to create a buffer zone of independent states around Germany, to prevent future territorial expansion, were the primary forces in the creation of independent Czechoslovakia, Poland, Hungary, Yugoslovia, and Austria. The Treaty of Versailles ratified the creation of these new states as well as officially ending World War 1.

The principalities of Bohemia, Moravia, Slovakia, and Ruthenia became the Republic of Czechoslovakia on October 28, 1918. The new state was formally created with the signing of the Treaty of St. Germaine, in September, 1919. A provisional government, supported by all Czech and Slovak political parties, governed the new state until the first election. A constitution for the new state was proclaimed in February, 1920, and the first democratic election was held the following April.

Czech politicians and intellectuals, in exile in western Europe, were the driving force behind the establishment of the Czechoslovak republic through the Czech National Council. Council members were either ignorant of, or oblivious to, the objections of the Sudeten German population living in the territory proposed for the republic. Sudeten Germans demonstrated throughout the Sudetenland in March, 1919, to protest their being included in the Republic of Czechoslovakia. These people wanted self-determination, which meant being granted their request to become citizens of independent Austria.

Although these demonstrations in the Sudeten German cities were conducted in a peaceful manner, in a number of cities a trigger-happy Czech army fired into the demonstrators. Fifty-four demonstrators were killed and several hundred wounded. The protests failed and the Sudeten Germans became an ethnic minority within the Czechoslovak state.

Difficult economic, political, and social problems faced the new state almost immediately. The new state had acquired the industrial heartland of the old empire but had lost the large internal market served by this industry. The glassware and textiles produced in Czechoslovakia were forced to compete in the export market with similar products from other newly independent states. To add to the problem of market loss, the value established for the Czechoslovak crown was high, relative to other European currencies. Czechoslovakian export products were expensive in a competitive market with the result that buyers for these products were even more difficult to find. Industrial production dropped and wages remained low. Unemployment and poverty became major social and political problems in the industrial regions.

The German population had reluctantly accepted becoming part of the Czech state in the belief that the various ethnic minorities would have local autonomy within a state modelled after Switzerland. The Swiss model provided for national self-determination within regions, local power over education and administration, and state control over foreign affairs and the economy. This state organization was not introduced and the minority questions were initially ignored.

The language law, proclaimed as part of the Czechoslovak constitution, declared the Czech language to be the only official language. Civil servants were required to pass Czech language examinations to qualify for employment. This legislation was deeply resented by the Sudeten Germans. Dismissal of several thousand state employees, postal officials and railway workers unable to speak the language, increased the economic problems and bitterness of the German population. Political and social conflicts between the two ethnic groups arose again over the language of the courts, the administration, and the school system. Czech soldiers, returning from service in a border dispute between Poland and Russia, staged anti-German demonstrations in the Sudetenland, destroying monuments of symbolic importance to the Sudeten Germans. Sudeten Germans objected to the building of Czech schools, when schools were not provided for German minorities. Democrats of both ethnic groups worked to reduce friction but nationalistic interests continued to divide the political and social life of the population.

Economic problems were overcome as markets were found in postwar Europe and North America for the industrial products of Czechoslovakia. Political problems were reduced by the improved economy and by the establishment of several political parties representing ideological and ethnic minorities. Under the multi-party system no single party gained an absolute majority; therefore, coalitions among the parties formed the state governments between 1920 and 1938. Social problems were reduced by the economic improvement and the diversity of political representation in government. The formation of trade unions had helped to overcome low wages and poor working conditions for both Czech and German workers. Trade union ideology was translated into political activity through the Social Democratic and Communist parties.

In the election of 1925, the Czech and German social democratic parties lost ground and paved the way for a right of center coalition. The new coalition included, for the first time, members of two German parties: the Federation of Farmers and the Christian Social Party. The election in 1929 saw the two social democratic parties regain strength and the German Social Democratic Party became a member of the coalition. Then the coalition included three German cabinet ministers to speak for the Sudeten German population, and work toward a solution of their grievances.

The promise of a gradual solution to the internal problems of Czechoslovakia in the 1920's fell apart when events outside the state dragged its problems into the center of European politics. World-wide economic depression followed the 1929 New York stockmarket crash. The highly industrialized Sudetenland bore the brunt of Czechoslovakian unemployment. Unemployment figures from 1938 show 9.1 percent of the Czech and Slovak work force unemployed when

38.7 percent of the German work force were out of work. In 1933 Hitler came to power in Germany and began a propaganda campaign directed toward the unemployed Sudeten Germans. Nazi radio commentary blamed the democratic government of Czechoslovakia for high unemployment and boasted of the reduction in unemployment in Germany. Sudeten Germans, desperate for work, crossed the border to find jobs in Germany while maintaining their homes in Czechoslovakia. One of the conditions of employment in Germany was membership in the National Socialist Party.

Nazi ideology had been represented in Czechoslovakia by a National Socialist Party; however, before being outlawed the party voluntarily dissolved in 1933. German nationalist sentiment was then represented by several smaller political parties which reorganized into the Sudeten German Party under the leadership of Konrad Henlein. The Sudeten German Party gained strength with the behind-the-scenes support of the German Nazi party. The inability of the Czechoslovakian state government to develop a positive plan to overcome the economic problems of the industrial regions or solve the cultural problems of its German-speaking citizens turned many Sudeten Germans away from democracy. In the election of 1935 Sudeten German representation in parliament went overwhelmingly to the Sudeten German party. The party elected forty-four out of a possible seventy representatives. The Social Democrats, Christian Socialists and Farmers parties held the remaining seats as representatives of the German-speaking population. The structure of the coalition government remained unchanged as the Sudeten German Party did not join the coalition. The government recognized that Sudeten German dissatisfaction had grown and efforts had to be made to meet their demands.

Following the dramatic decline in support for the other German parties in the election, a movement began to bring new, younger men into the party leadership. Both the Federation of Farmers and Christian Socialist parties elected young leaders. These men joined the young vice chairman of the German Social Democratic Party, Wenzel Jaksch, to work out a common platform for settlement of the national problems. This group became known as the Young Activists. They announced their proposals in April, 1936 and opened an office in Prague, from which negotiations with sympathetic Czech groups began. Their efforts bore fruit when, on February 18, 1937, Prime Minister Hodža announced acceptance of compromise resolutions for Sudeten German grievances. These resolutions were known as the February 18 Agreement.

The resolutions promised wide ranging changes in policy regarding investment in the Sudeten German districts hardest hit by the depression. In the fields of social welfare and health, the government promised to establish aid programs on the basis of district unemployment figures rather than population. Special attention was also promised for the catastrophic number of unemployed young people. It was agreed to relax the stringent Czech language tests in the regulations for civil service jobs. It was promised that official correspondence with the state, in districts where non-Czechs were in the majority, would be handled in the majority language. The German school system, which had suffered from the closing of over four thousand classrooms since 1918, was to receive government assistance. Aid was also promised to other minorities for the purpose of education. Where the interests of national minorities were not specifically upheld in practice, the government promised to see that unjust administrative regulations were changed.

The February 18 Agreement gave new hope to the democrats among the Sudeten Germans. The words of the agreement sounded wonderful but putting the words into practice went too slowly and began too late. During the first year about 6,000 jobs were created in minority districts suffering most from the depression. These jobs, however, did not even make a dent in the economic situation of the more than half a million unemployed Sudeten Germans.

When Hitler occupied Austria in March, 1938 the impact on the German political parties in Czechoslovaki was so great, and the Sudeten German Party so strong, that the Christian Socialist Party and Farmers Party joined the Sudeten German Party. The coalition government fell apart and the German Social Democratic Party was dismissed from the coalition.

Czech and German democrats still tried to convince the government that self-determination for the German-speaking population within the state would strengthen democracy and the resistance to Nazi ideology. After Hitler occupied Austria in 1938 outside pressure on the government to settle the problems of the Sudeten Germans increased. Czechoslovakia's ally, France, backed by her ally, Britain, urged the hesitant government to make a decision, as they feared military invasion from Germany would force them into an unnecessary full scale war. Following British Prime Minister Chamberlain's meeting with Hitler in mid-September 1938, and his now foolish "peace in our time" statement, Britain and France decided the fate of the Sudeten Germans at a conference in Munich. The Munich Agreement signed by the leaders of Britain, France, Germany, and Italy ceded the Sudetenland, with its population, (Appendix 1) to Nazi Germany. The occupation was to begin October 1, 1938, and be completed by October 10, 1938. A plebiscite was to be held among the German-speaking population of the interior to determine whether they would move to German held territory or remain Czech citizens. The new border of Czechoslovakia was guaranteed by the four major powers.

Many thousands of people fled the Sudetenland including supporters of the German Social Democratic Party, other anti-Nazis, and Jews. Some anti-Nazis, unable to flee, were arrested by the occupying army and taken to Germany. Others took their own lives. An estimated 20,000 German Social Democrats were interned in concentration camps, such as Dachau. Between 30,000 and 50,000 Sudeten German Democrats fled to the interior of Czechoslovakia and became refugees in their own country.

2

BECOMING POLITICAL REFUGEES

When 1938 began, I was district secretary for the German Social Democratic Party in Asch. As a full-time employee of the party I was responsible for party organization in the district. This area was a small peninsula of the border land in north-western Czechoslovakia surrounded by Germany. The region was hilly and covered with trees. Most of the people worked in the textile and glove making factories. They lived in small villages or in apartments in the town of Asch. Few people owned their own homes or much property. The people who lived in the villages often saved for many years before they could afford to build a small brick house. Factory owners or managers and some local business men lived in individual houses, but the working majority lived in small buildings of two or three apartments. Many people had become unemployed when the depression hit, and were dependent on financial assistance from trade unions, the state, or political parties.

Politically, the people of Asch supported various political parties, with the Communists and Social Democrats receiving most of the industrial workers' support. An election was called in May, 1938, and all of the German-speaking population of Czechoslovakia felt heavy pressure from the Nazi sponsored Sudeten German Party. The Sudeten German Party had consistently denied its link with Nazi Germany stating that its major concern was the equality and self-determination of the German-speaking citizens of Czechoslovakia. During the election campaign the Sudeten German Party published an eight point proposal for the solution of problems between the Czech and German populations. One of the points demanded was the right to openly support German political philosophy.

This was the first public admission that the real political philosophy of the party was the same as Hitler's National Socialist Party. Our Social Democratic party had had information confirming the Nazi connection to the Sudeten German party for some time. I personally had known of the link since shortly after I moved to Asch in 1933. Konrad Henlein, the leader of the Sudeten German Party lived in Asch and I was aware of his activities. Through friendship with Czech border guards and German Social Democrats who had fled Germany, I learned that Henlein frequently crossed the border to meet with Nazi party officials in Germany. The Sudeten German people were deceived by Henlein and his lavish campaign and promises to fight for their self-determination. They did not realize that democracy was threatened, and refused to listen to the warnings of other political parties.

An experience I had during the 1938 municipal election campaign illustrates the changed sentiment of the people of Asch. I returned to town early one evening after attending a political rally in an outlying village. When I came into town many people, mostly working people, were lined up along the main street. The women were carrying flowers. As I rode my bicycle along the street they spit at me and called me a "bonze," which means someone who is wealthy and leads a luxurious life. I had to run the gauntlet along that street to reach my office. After I cleaned up from this unpleasant experience I could hear the crowd chanting "Henlein, Henlein." I looked out the window and saw Konrad Henlein coming down the main street in a fine black Mercedes Benz with several other cars behind his. The women who had spit at me earlier were throwing flowers at him and cheering. No one called him a "bonze" yet he lived in an eleven room villa and had two expensive cars, while I lived in a two room apartment and rode a bicycle. Among the people who lined the streets I could recognize some who had supported the Social Democratic Party in the past because of our programs and philosophy, but were now beguiled by the expensive cars and display which covered the Nazi political philosophy.

In the election our party gained a respectable percentage of the vote because many who feared losing their jobs did not openly support us, but voted for us. However, the Sudeten

German Party received the majority of votes in the Sudetenland and most municipal governments were under their control.

Shortly after the election Konrad Henlein visited England to meet with government leaders. He presented his proposals for solution of the problems of Czechoslovak German-speaking citizens. British officials were impressed with Henlein, who appeared to be an honest representative of the Sudeten Germans and sincerely interested in a speedy settlement of the problem. Henlein's personality and proposals obscured the threat to Czechoslovak democracy and the lives of anti-Nazis. Britain and France began to pressure the Czechoslovak government to settle the Sudeten German problem by granting local autonomy to the predominately German-speaking districts within the state. The leaders of western European countries were reluctant to become involved in a full scale war to protect minority rights in Czechoslovakia when reasonable internal solutions were available. The Czech government rejected these proposals while granting some concessions to the German-speaking population. The Sudeten German Party leaders were unwilling to accept these concessions without autonomy: the Czech government was unwilling to grant autonomy. Tension between the anti-Nazi and Nazi groups grew as negotiations continued throughout the summer between the government and the Sudeten German Party. In September the situation exploded into violent demonstrations in many German-speaking districts.

Hitler made an hysterical speech in Nuremberg on September 12, 1938 which in turn touched off widespread Nazi demonstrations in the Sudetenland. Angry crowds smashed the windows of Jewish shops, attacked known anti-Nazis and took over post offices, police posts, and customs offices. Those who resisted were beaten; some were killed. The Czech government declared martial law in the Sudetenland in an attempt to control the demonstrations. The districts of Asch and Eger were hard hit by this violence. People who feared for their lives because of their known opposition to the Nazis began leaving their homes for refuge in the interior districts.

A Czech army commander from the nearest garrison in Eger had told me earlier that the district of Asch was considered indefensible by the Czech army. He advised me to leave if trouble started. Demonstrations in Asch began while I was out in the district checking to see what effect Hitler's speech might have had on the people of the area. While I was away one of the militia members who knew where I was phoned me and told me not to come into Asch on the main street. He told me that demonstrations were going on and windows were being smashed by the Nazis. I planned to avoid the main street when I returned, but in one of the villages just outside Asch a cordon of men blocked the road. They were dressed in high boots and brown shirts and signaled with their hands for me to stop. I was riding a motorcycle and pretended to stop. Just as I was about to stop, and close enough to recognize the men in the cordon, I put on full gas and rode right through them. They jumped aside and fell into the ditch. Some of them fired their pistols at me, but I was not hit. I managed to get to my office in the party auditorium building without encountering more Nazis. I realized I could not go home through the demonstrators, so I stayed overnight in my office.

Early the next morning the government representative in Asch told me that he could not guarantee my safety as he did not have enough policemen. He told me that the Henlein supporters would take over control of the town at noon, and advised me to get out as quickly as possible. I told him I could not leave as long as I had party members in the district, and that I could not notify them all to get out in such a short time. He promised me that the police outposts would notify my people, in the outlying areas, who could not be reached by telephone. He kept his promise. Party members throughout the district were notified of the takeover and many began to leave.

I started cleaning out my office and burning documents. The secretary of the textile workers union Karl Parthe helped me, but when noon came we were still not finished. A rumor about the contents of large crates I had helped unload protected us from the Nazi forces taking over the town. The crates had contained the costumes of a theater group not guns. The rumor was false but when a Nazi came to the office, while we were still working, I implied that we were armed and prepared to deal with him and his kind. The office was not attacked because the Nazis were not sure whether we were armed or not and decided not to find out.

By evening we had completed our work, but we knew the Nazis had barricaded the streets to prevent people leaving. I was still wearing my black leather outfit which I wore when riding my motorcycle, and looked like an SS man. My appearance helped me to escape. A friend went into the street to get a taxi. When the taxi arrived it was driven by a uniformed Nazi. My friend got in beside the driver and gave directions while I got into the back seat without speaking. When we came to the barricades they thought we were Nazis and waved us through. The Czech army had also set up barricades and when they saw the Nazi uniforms they stopped the car. I then showed my identification and we were waved on to Eger. Only when I stepped out of the car in Eger did the driver realize who had been his passenger. I was fairly certain he would never admit to what he had done, but said to him: "You won't say who you drove out when you go back will you?" He was silent. I gave him some money and went to the military garrison. The next day I left with some other party members, who had also escaped, to go to the army garrison at Mies. The military commander there told me, a few days later, that tanks and men from Eger had gone into Asch and were in control. The Nazis had gone. I thought it was a chance to return to Asch to see what had actually happened. I went back and spent a few days getting more people out, because I was sure the Nazis would return. When I reached Asch, I telephoned party headquarters in Prague. Headquarters officials were relieved to learn I was still alive, but I caught hell because I had gone back to Asch and was told to leave immediately. I stayed until September 21, 1938 when I left permanently.

When I reached Prague I learned that British Prime Minister Neville Chamberlain had flown to Berchtesgaden to meet Adolf Hitler to discuss the Sudeten German problem. Hitler had demanded that the Sudetenland be given to Germany or he would take it by force. I also learned that Chamberlain, and the Premier of France, Edouard Daladier, had proposed that Germany be given Czechoslovak territory where more than fifty percent of the people were German speaking. Czech President Beneš, and his cabinet, rejected the proposal. Their decision was firmly supported by the German Social Democrats and Czech political parties. Through the British and French embassies in Prague further pressure was applied to give up the territory. Public opinion was against any action to allow Germany to occupy Czechoslovak territory. The Czech people and the Sudeten German democrats were willing to fight for their state rather than surrender to Hitler's demands.

President Beneš resigned September 22, 1938, choosing an army general as his successor. The new president, General Jan Syrový, called for full mobilization of the Czech army. The mobilization order was willingly obeyed by Sudeten Germans, as a similar order in May had been obeyed. The majority of the conscripts could have easily escaped across the German border, but they did not. Sudeten German willingness to obey the mobilization order was a more important demonstration of their support for a democratic state than their support for the Sudeten German Party in the May election.

In a radio speech, announcing the establishment of military rule, President Beneš had stated that he had a plan. He did not elaborate. No one knew whether he was going to give a belated call for resistance or announce the worst: total surrender. When the mobilization order came, it was assumed by most people that Czechoslovakia would resist the Nazi threat with the help of her allies, France and Britain.

The German Social Democratic Party had arranged a conference in Prague to discuss the grave political situation and to work out a plan for the struggle against the growing threats of the Nazis toward our country and our freedom. Our agenda also included the problem of inequality. Czechoslovakia had not treated its minorities in an evenhanded way and had not given us the feeling of equal citizenship in this Versailles and St. Germain-created country. Inequality and unfairness were particularly obvious in employment practices, the letting of government contracts, and cultural matters. Sudeten German Social Democrats stood on the side of the state and were willing to die for it because we knew that eventually we would achieve equality. We were willing to be patient as we had confidence that the programs, agreed to before the threat of Nazi takeover, would eliminate many inequities if given time to take effect and reach the people most concerned. At that conference we chose to remain loyal to the Czechoslovak government and continued to be their ally in the struggle against Nazism. We Sudeten German Social Democrats were the best allies the Czechoslovak government had ever had since the state had come into existence.

During the deliberations at our conference the news reached us that the western powers would most likely give in to Hitler's demands in the hope of avoiding war. This news had a very disheartening effect on us, giving us a feeling of utter frustration. We could not believe, after all the previous experiences with Hitler, that the western powers would desert their close and faithful ally, Czechoslovakia, and throw this last democracy in Central Europe to the Nazi wolves without a fight. Our trust in the western powers had been shaken by the coups Hitler had effected, but never had we thought about the possibility of Czechoslovakia falling into Nazi hands. I vividly recall the party leader, Wenzel Jaksch, standing on the platform shouting to us, and to the world, "There must be a place somewhere in the world — be it in the forests of Canada — where Sudeten German Social Democrats, who are prepared to risk their life for freedom, can find protection and a life in freedom." Behind this desperate outcry from our party leader there was no plan for escape. The possibility of flight had not previously been considered. The remaining time, at the conference, was spent developing an emergency escape plan to be set in motion if the western powers agreed to Hitler's terms.

Czechoslovakia's fate was determined in meetings attended by the leaders of Britain, France, Italy, and Germany, held in Munich. Final agreement was reached and announced on September 29, 1938. The Sudetenland, its population, military installations, and communication links were to be transferred to Germany. The German-speaking population of the interior districts were to decide whether to move to German held territory or remain in Czechoslovakia. A plebiscite, supervised by an international commission, would be held to record their decision. There was no plebiscite because Hitler never honored that part of the Munich agreement. The transfer was to begin October 1 and be completed by October 10, 1938. Without firing a single shot, Adolf Hitler was given what he had demanded!

On his return to London, following the Munich conference, Mr. Chamberlain stepped off the plane and declared before a cheering crowd: "My good friends, this is the second time in history that there has come back from Germany, to Downing Street, peace with honor. I believe it is peace for our time, and now I recommend you go home and sleep quietly in your beds." In the four days of debate in the British House of Commons following the Munich Agreement not all members of the Chamberlain government shared their leader's confidence in his policy of appeasement. Duff Cooper, first Lord of the Admiralty, and Foreign Secretary, Anthony Eden, resigned in protest. Winston Churchill said, "This is only the first sip, the first bitter foretaste of a bitter cup which will be proffered to us..." Few people listened to the protests of these men. The mass of British people honestly believed in Mr. Chamberlain's "peace in our time" statement. The thought of war over three and one half million Sudeten Germans who, in the words of Lord Runciman, a British observer in Prague, "wanted to go home to the Reich", did not justify the sacrifice of a single British soldier in their minds.

The capitulation of the western powers at the Munich conference was a stunning blow to Sudeten German anti-Nazis. It put us in a very uncertain situation and it was not clear whether the Czech government would protect us. The Czech Agrarian Party newspaper **Venkov** declared: "We alone must now build a pure national state. From now on we will be alone. Our former humanity will have to cease. Foreigners need not expect consideration from our people." The anti-Nazi Germans were then certain that there was little hope left for them. They packed up what belongings they could carry and rushed to catch the last trains which would take them to the interior of the country and perhaps refuge. The general withdrawal of the Czech army from the Sudetenland had also begun. Before Hitler's occupation troops crossed into the Sudetenland the roads and trains were jammed with troops and civilians leaving. When groups of anti-Nazi refugees reached safety, in the interior districts, they were told by Czech authorities to go back to their homes and vote in the plebiscite. The refugees from the Sudetenland, who found temporary refuge in the interior of Czechoslovakia, were trapped. Poland and Hungary occupied other border districts of Czechoslovakia and effectively blocked all escape routes from the country.

After the party conference, I had remained in Prague to work as a volunteer at party headquarters. The emergency plans developed at the conference were put into operation and it was my job to help sift out those who were not actually endangered political refugees but were trying to sneak into our rescue operations. While in the office in Prague I learned that Czech soldiers had rounded up a large number of people in Pilzen, and were forcing them to board trains bound for Asch. I rushed out of Prague on my motorcycle to try to stop that expulsion, with the help of some Czech members of parliament. When I arrived in Pilzen I was told that the train had already left. Depressed and furious I returned to Prague. The Czech authorities had set up road blocks on the outskirts of the city to prevent an influx of refugees. Fortunately, I had a document certifying that I worked in our party headquarters or I would have been refused re-entry to the city. It was becoming obvious that some circles of the Czech Agrarian Party, which dominated the government in Prague, were trying to please Berlin. This was, I believe, the only explanation for the unfriendly act of expelling refugees, the same people who had stood on the borders prepared to fight for the country if that fight had come.

A few days later I received an order from the police to leave Prague within three days or be forcibly returned to Asch. The order had been authorized by the Czech Agrarian Minister of Interior, Dr. Černy. I do not know the real reason I received that order but I have always suspected that someone in the Prague government was trying to do the Nazis a favor. I had known for some time that I was on the Nazi blacklist for the help I had given the German underground in Asch. I admit that I was pretty desperate as I had a good idea of what I would have to face if the Gestapo caught me.

I showed the order to Siegfried Taub, First Secretary of the Sudeten German Social Democratic Party and Vice President of parliament. He said he would speak to the Minister. He tried to do so at once but could not reach him.

The next morning it was the same. When I had only twenty-four hours left, before my expulsion, I called on the Chinese Ambassador, Dr. Lionel Liang, whom I had known from one of his lecture tours. The Ambassador said that he would like to help me but could not see how he could get me out of the country. He could not, even as a friend, recommend his country as a refuge for me as the situation there was not very likely to make it a safe place to stay.

When I left the Chinese Embassy I made up my mind that I would not leave Prague. I returned to the office where I was told that there was still no word from the Czech authorities on my situation. At the last minute Mr. Taub told me he could take me to his home. There I would be safe until matters concerning my stay in Prague could be resolved. Policemen were not allowed to enter the home of a member of parliament.

The next day Mr. Taub reached the responsible Minister. One hour before my time to stay expired, a phone call came from the Minister stating that my expulsion order was rescinded. I was to report to the chief of police in the city district where I lived to pick up a certificate for my stay in Prague. I went to the police station and to my surprise the police chief had known me from the time he had been chief of the state police in Asch. Now that so many years have passed, I feel free to repeat what that man said to me after he listened to my story. He said, "If that swine of a Minister had carried out this order and I had heard about it I would have shot him." With a friend of that caliber in Prague, my worries were over. Not only that, I was also able to be of help to some of our people who had similar difficulties.

We became political refugees when the western powers abandoned their principles by cooperating with the ruthless regime in Germany, at the signing of the Munich Agreement, and when we were refused sanctuary by the government to which we had remained loyal. Our only crime, as Sudeten German democrats, was that we refused to relinquish, without resistance, the rights of free speech, free association, and humane government. Our resistance to fascist dictatorship, and the fact that we had helped political refugees from Germany and Austria, would have weighed heavily on us if we had been captured by the Gestapo. We fled, although we did not know where to go. We knew that the rump state of Czechoslovakia would, most likely, not be willing or able to absorb the thousands of refugees from the Sudetenland. We must escape and leave our homeland, perhaps forever.

3

WITH THE HELP OF FRIENDS

The plans for emergency escape, made during the German Social Democratic Party Conference, went into operation as soon as the terms of the Munich Agreement were known. Money had to be raised to pay for food and shelter for the people fleeing to the interior. Visas had to be obtained from western countries for entry and stay. As most of the refugees were penniless and some had no winter clothing, money for transportation and clothing had to be found. It was a monumental task, which we would never have been able to master without the help of friends in a number of countries. Our problems were made more difficult by the policy of the Czech government regarding our citizenship.

The Czech government was in a state of disarray, struggling for survival, and would do nothing for us which could cause disfavor with its adversaries abroad, especially in Berlin. After the signing of the Munich Agreement, Dr. Černy, Minister of Internal Affairs, claimed that, by this Agreement, all residents of the ceded territory automatically became citizens of Germany. He argued that it was not his responsibility to issue passports to us. He refused to accept our claims that we were citizens of Czechoslovakia, and that we no longer lived in the districts ceded to Germany, which gave us the right to our original citizenship. We had demonstrated, by our move into the remaining parts of Czechoslovakia, that we did not want citizenship in Nazi Germany, but wanted to remain citizens of Czechoslovakia. Before we could start getting visas the position taken by the Czech government had to be reversed.

Our members of parliament, who were still our legal representatives, finally worked out a compromise with the Minister after the Czech counterpart of our party added their strength to our requests. The compromise made it possible for us to obtain interim passports. These passports were legal for emigration, but not for return to Czechoslovakia. Since a passport was a requirement for a visa, we had no choice but to accept this shameful document.

While the negotiations were going on some of our members, with valid passports, were flown out of the country as soon as the first visas were granted by Britain and Sweden. This procedure was used to avoid the loss of a single valuable visa, which had to be used within a specified time limit. However, obtaining passports and visas for our people, waiting in camps under poor conditions, was a slow time-consuming process.

The attitude of the Czech government was not shared by all Czech people. Many individuals in government gave us a helping hand where they could. The President of the Senate, Dr. František Soukup, was an outstanding example. He offered his office to a Norwegian delegation which had come to Prague to help in solving our problems. The most understanding people, among the Czech population , were people who had lived in the Sudeten districts, like my friend the police chief. These people had seen the heroic stand taken by the Sudeten German anti-Nazis and the abuse they had endured. Organizations offered meeting halls and gymnasiums as shelter for the refugees. I visited a camp in Beroun, which had been set up in the Czech Athletic Association hall. There was some straw on the floor and a few people had some blankets, but everyone slept on the floor. A primitive kitchen had been set up for cooking. There were many camps similar to this throughout the interior of Czechoslovakia.

The planning and coordination of our emigration was directed and supervised by the party leader and executive from party headquarters in Prague. The staff and many volunteers worked around the clock attending to the thousands of details and problems of the operation. When interim passports became available, volunteers spent many hours completing passport applications. Only a few among our refugees had passports. Many of our refugees were without the personal documents necessary to obtain a passport. That obstacle could be overcome if our party established the identity of a refugee and gave the applicant a certificate signed by an official of the party. After certificates were issued, passport application forms had to be taken to the various refugee camps to be filled out and supported by the required documents.

Our party leader, Wenzel Jaksch, with his interpreter, Willi Wanka, had flown to London on October 1, 1938, to seek help for the many thousands of refugees who were trapped in the remaining parts of Czechoslovakia. In London, they went knocking on the doors of influential people requesting help in getting people out of the country and supplying those in refugees camps with food. Their task was made somewhat easier by the reports from journalists in Prague. The British press had sent reporters to Prague, and they had started to report on the plight of our refugees. This helped our envoys to open doors and ears in England, giving us hope that a way out would be found.

The diplomatic correspondent of the **Daily Telegraph** reported on October 3, 1938, that: "Reliable reports estimated the number of Germans, who are opponents of Nazism, to be 400,000. They are those who do not wish to leave their homes and places of employment in the districts of the Sudetenland."

Mr. Seton-Watson and Blanche Dugvale wrote in the same edition of the same newspaper: "Besides 400,000 Czechs, an estimated 100,000 democratic-minded Germans and between 20,000 and 30,000 Jews fled into the interior of Czechoslovakia. Thousands of them have exposed themselves to the vengeance of the Nazis and can never return to the ceded districts."

The following day, the Prague correspondent of the **London News Chronicle** reported to his paper: "Reports from the Sudeten districts, which are occupied by the Germans now, are speaking of the suicide of hundreds of families. Fathers killed their children and the parents committed suicide not to have to live under the Nazi yoke. Also, here in Prague, many cases of suicide have been reported, especially among the Sudeten German refugees, who were forced to return to the occupied former home districts, in which their fate would be sealed. Reports about hangings and tortures in the Sudetenland are already leaking through. Leaders of the Social Democratic Party, who did not succeed in their escape — and many who refused to leave their home — were without bother murdered or handed over to the Gestapo for 'treatment', which is worse than death."

The **News Chronicle** in another report about the plight of the Sudeten German refugees noted that: "The German refugees are indeed more to feel sorry for than the Czechs. The latter have at least a homeland where they can go, the Sudeten Germans have none."

The **News Chronicle**, which repeatedly championed the right of protection for the Sudeten German refugees, appealed in an article on October 6, 1938, for financial help and continued: "Alarming reports about the terrible suffering of the refugees are coming uninterrupted to Prague. Under the pressure of threats from Germany, the Czechs will not take any more refugees. Many refugees are stranded between the German-Czech lines and are exposed to the attacks of the Henlein people.

"In Tetschen-Bodenbach, German soldiers were forced to shoot three of those Henlein people for looting. In the castle of Count Thun, in Tetschen, the first concentration camp for German anti-Nazis was opened. According to reports, shots can be heard from this castle day and night." (Two Sudeten German escapees reported later in London that in the case of Count Thun's castle no mass executions took place, thanks to a German army general who protected the prisoners from the Gestapo.)

In another report in the same edition the **News Chronicle** reported: "As soon as the Czech troops withdrew from these districts the armed FS people (Nazis) rounded up all the people who had been advised by the Czech authorities to stay for voting in the plebiscite. Democrats were picked up in their homes and even dragged from their motorcycles. Their further fate is unknown.

"Today a trainload of 1,000 of these unfortunate people, including women and children, were transported from Pilzen back to Asch."

Sir Walter Layton, publisher of the **News Chronicle**,

established the Fund for the Refugees from Czechoslovakia, and appealed in his newspaper for donations. Sir Henry Twyford made a public appeal on October 5, 1938, for establishing the Lord Mayor of London Fund for Refugees from Czechoslovakia. These funds played an important role in financing the support of our refugees in camps in England and other countries, and covering the cost of visas and transportation.

Thanks to the press, the conscience of the British public was aroused to the plight of the Sudeten German refugees. Pressure to do something positive, such as at least grant some visas, mounted on the Chamberlain government. A delegation from the British Labor Party headed by Mr. Green and Mr. Dallas, both members of the House of Commons, intervened on our behalf on October 13, 1938, at the Foreign Office and Dominion Ministry. Only two days later the Liberal leader, Mr. Wick, spoke in support of the Sudeten German refugees at a public meeting in his constituency: "The Czechs are afraid to accept them because they are afraid that Germany would demand more of their country's territory, and afraid that the government of Germany had not given up its demand for all Germans." Mr. Wick ended his speech with an appeal for help for the refugees. British Labor Party leader, Clement Attlee, and Mr. Hugh Dalton pressed repeatedly in the House of Commons for help in the matter. On October 18, 1938, Labor M.P., David R. Grenfell, demanded immediate help for us, and on the same day the Foreign Office granted the first 300 visas for the Sudeten German refugees.

Unfortunately, the visas issued by the Chamberlain government admitted only men refugees. The policy was finally changed after political and public opinion mounted against this discrimination. Miss Rathbone, an independent member of the British parliament, questioned Mr. Chamberlain in the House of Commons about this policy. Mr. Chamberlain then promised that the families of men refugees would be permitted entry if the means for their support could be obtained. Miss Doreen Warriner, a member of the British Labor Party, who had voluntarily come to Prague to help us, also had a hand in assuring that visas were granted for the entire family rather than just for men.

Representatives from other European countries came to Prague to aid our rescue operation. Axel Granath, secretary of the Swedish Arbetarroerelsens Flyktinghjaelp (Refugee Assistance of the Labor Movement), received a call from Prague for help. He flew to Czechoslovakia at once to see what had to be done. Three other members of the Swedish labor movement arrived shortly after Granath. They promised to do their utmost to find refuge for a number of people in Sweden and other northern countries. They kept their promise. Fin Moe, foreign policy expert with the Norwegian trade union movement, and a police official, Mr. Konstadt, arrived in Prague to help us. Mr. Troels Hoff and Richard Hansen, members of the Refugee Committee of the Danish Social Democratic Party, also came to Prague.

While admittance to England was dependent on available finance for the support of the refugees, in Norway and Denmark the parliaments set the number of persons who were to be admitted. In Sweden, on the other hand, the administration of the Refugee Assistance Committee decided how many refugees could be supported.

Parliament, in Copenhagen, acted swiftly when Mr. Troels Hoff came back from Prague and reported on the situation there. When some members of parliament were discussing whether or not some refugees should be admitted, the Conservative leader, Mr. Mowinkel, intervened and said, "In this matter there is no discussion necessary, let's vote." That done Mr. Hoff could make the decision, and he accepted the first list of refugees, handed to him in Prague, for immediate consideration.

Norway, with a small population was, like Sweden, caring for many refugees from Austria and Germany and was not able to accept a great number of us. About sixty found at least a temporary home in Norway until the German invasion, then they had to flee again. Some who did not succeed in escaping to Sweden fell into the hands of the Gestapo and were sent to concentration camps. The same happened in Finland, when the small number of our refugees who had found asylum there had to flee again when the German army came to Finland to attack Russia from that front. Again, when Denmark was invaded, the refugees had to flee: Some reached England via

Sweden, and the remainder were allowed to stay in Sweden.

Belgium, which was a very delicate country because of the large number of refugees it already supported, yielded to desperate calls for help and granted seventy-five entry visas. Another seventy-five visas were issued later, on the condition that the stay of the refugees would only be temporary. But the pressure in Prague, to speed up the departure of refugees, increased. By March 1939, about 300 refugees found temporary accommodation in Belgium, when the Belgian Refugee Committee received financial assistance from England.

The countries of western Europe did not all respond sympathetically to our problem. The case of France was a very sad one. The French Foreign Minister, George Bonnet, had promised the Vice Chairman of the Foreign Relations Committee, Mr. Solomon Grumbach, member of the French parliament, and champion of our cause in France, that 700 entry visas would be granted, and that instructions, to that effect, would be given to the French Embassy in Prague. Every day our Senator, Dr. Heller, went to the French Embassy to ask whether or not these instructions had been received from Paris. And every day he got the same answer: No. Then the news came from our representative in Paris, Mr. Leopold Goldschmidt, that the intervention of Mr. Grumbach had been successful. The news brought joy and immediate action in our Prague office. Ernst Paul worked almost around the clock to put a list of 700 refugees together, and to get them through the cumbersome process for emigration, in order to have them ready for departure when the promised visas arrived. When nothing happened, our friends in Paris again put pressure on the French authorities. But what we finally got were 100 visas for only temporary stay in France. The refugees who had been assigned to the French visas had to be moved on to other countries. That was the "help" from a country whose Prime Minister, Daladier, was a co-signer of the Munich Agreement, which had caused all the misery for us.

The failure of some western European governments to assist us was more than compensated for by the individuals who assisted us for humanitarian reasons. Mr. William Gilles, international secretary of the British Labor Party, came to Prague to get a personal look at the situation and helped obtain visas from his country for our refugees. Mr. Robert Stopford, a British liaison officer to the Czech government, proved himself very helpful in obtaining funds for the emigration of refugees. In Britain, Mrs. Minnie B. Theobald left a comfortable home in Brighton, to help the Sudeten refugees find places to stay. Other individuals, who had been closely associated with the decisions regarding the fate of the Sudetenland, were unwilling to help.

While in London Mr. Jaksch had been advised by Mr. Attlee to visit Lord Runciman. Runciman had been sent to Prague by Prime Minister Chamberlain, in the summer of 1938, to report on the political situation. Mr. Jaksch, a former member of a delegation of anti-Nazis, had tried to explain our position in the dispute and the cleverly fostered plans of the Sudeten German Party. Mr. Attlee felt that, since the Runciman report had been a factor in the British decision to sign the Munich Agreement, Lord Runciman would feel a certain responsibility to the victims of the Agreement, and would use his influence to help solve the visa problems. Mr. Jaksch reluctantly told me, several years later, that he had approached Lord Runciman for help. Lord Runciman had said he was a private person in Prague, and could not help, but that if the Lord Mayor of London created a fund for the refugees he would make a financial contribution. His answer had so angered Mr. Jaksch, that he told Lord Runciman bluntly that he had not come to him as a beggar for a token. Mr. Jaksch also told Runciman that he had expected him to use his influence to do a little more for the victims of his policy, because Runciman was partly responsible for the misery of the Sudeten German Social Democrats. Jaksch, and his interpreter, Willi Wanka, then left the office. Runciman followed them to offer some advice which, in the opinion of Mr. Jaksch, was as worthless as the report he had sent to the British government from Prague.

Even with the help received from friends in other countries, the main burden of the rescue operations remained on our party leader, Wenzel Jaksch, and the two first secretaries, Siegfried Taub and Ernst Paul. Jaksch commuted between London and Prague acting as our liaison with the British government and administrators of the refugee funds.

Taub worked with the administrative circles of the Czech government, trying to resolve the many political and personal problems of our emigration, such as arranging transportation when visas became available.

Transportation was a serious problem. Air transport could not be used for financial reasons even if all the refugees had been in possession of passports. At that time mass transport by air still had a long way to go. There were no 747's, or even planes of the 707 category, which could move thousands of people quickly. Therefore, other means of transportation, mostly trains and ships, had to be organized to move people.

Poland was the only land route leading to the free West. But that country, with its uncertain relations with Hitler, required transit permission for people passing through on the way to the port of Gdynia. Obtaining this permission was often impossible without the help of friendly governments.

The situation, in Prague, in the fall and winter of 1938-39, was best summed up in a letter written to a friend in Sweden, in April 1971, by Alois Mollik, one of the volunteer workers:

"Now we had to execute the technical part of the Jaksch-Taub action. This required understanding on the part of our bureaucrats in the various departments of the ministries in Prague. In an unobtrusive way they were made to understand that the abnormal conditions required special treatment. Time was of extreme importance.

"The procuring of passports, visas, tickets for the trains, airplanes, ships; booking of special trains, getting foreign exchange necessary for travel to foreign countries, which would normally have taken days or weeks, must sometimes be carried out within hours.

"The dispatch of transports up to the middle of December went very slowly and caused us to worry that the time we had left would not be sufficient.

"But what we wished became reality. Visas arrived and more transports at shorter intervals could be dispatched, taking more of our comrades out of the country......

"Sometimes we had only hours to organize people to avoid delaying the takeoff of a waiting plane. In most cases we just made it."

In the conclusion of his letter to his friend Mr. Mollik said; "Up to the invasion of Hitler's troops we had arranged that most of the people in the refugee camps could be brought out of the country. The evening of March 13, 1939, many left on the last organized special train. The ones still left behind found a guardian angel in Miss Doreen Warriner."

Those who were left behind were mainly women and children. They were the families of men who had been sent ahead to England, before family visas were obtained, or those who were still in the occupied districts and could not be cleared for entry to England with their husbands and fathers. Doreen Warriner, assisted by her two friends, Margaret Dougan and Beatrice Wellington, succeeded in bringing out 170 women and children right under the eyes of the German occupation forces in March 1939.

Thirty years later Miss Warriner wrote an account of the experiences she and her friends had had in 1939. It was printed in the **Sudeten Jahrbuch 1969**, published by **Die Bruecke** in Munich, Germany. The following excerpts, from that account, illustrate what these brave ladies had to face after the occupation of Prague by Hitler's troops and hordes of Nazi gestapo.

"I had in my care 170 women and children who were accommodated in six hotels: three groups in Chucle, two in Prague, and one group in the small Hotel Stern in Beroun. The longer their stay lasted, the more dangerous it became for the women, among them many who were known as anti-Henlein (Nazi) activists. Had we had permission for travel out of the country it would have been much simpler, and the chances of being found out by the gestapo would have been much less.

"The military authorities at the start did not have information about who was or was not an opponent of the Nazis and granted exit permits quite easily. Yes, even the gestapo could be influenced with bribes to obtain some exit permits. But a big sweep started and a new line of gestapo officials arrived. They went to work with their well-known thoroughness. The danger for my women refugees increased from day to day and I feared what would follow if the women should be discovered.

"After several attempts I succeeded in establishing some

liaison with the Czech police authorities, who promised to replace the passports which had fallen into the hands of the gestapo. That gave my women new hope. But then I received the crushing news: the gestapo got hold of the passports, which they would not release. Luckily we had money from the **News Chronicle** fund and at least could provide a roof over their heads and food for our women."

Further on Miss Warriner wrote in her account: "Totally unexpectedly the gestapo came to the hotel where Beatrice Wellington stayed. She was a Canadian who had left her employment in Geneva to come to Prague to assist me and Miss Dougan in our work for the Sudeten refugees. They took her to a gestapo office in Perstyn, a district in Prague, for interrogation. The gestapo wanted to know about the activity of our organization for help for the refugees.

"The Nazis were possessed by the wildest imaginations about our refugee assistance organization but after two hours of threats the gestapo learned nothing from Miss Wellington. They said that they would get her again next morning.

"Next morning an official of the British Consulate went to the hotel to give Miss Wellington assistance. He learned from the staff of the hotel that the gestapo had taken Miss Wellington out at six a.m. The British Consul wanted to know where Miss Wellington was taken. The gestapo lied to him and said that the Czech police had picked up Miss Wellington.

"The gestapo had taken Miss Wellington to a house outside of Prague and interrogated her in real Nazi-gestapo fashion for six hours trying to break her down. All during the six hours Miss Wellington had to stand while the gestapo threatened her and swore at her. But again she told them nothing about our work in Prague. That enraged her interrogators. They finally let Miss Wellington go and they were not any wiser after she had left than they were when they had brought her in."

The experiences of the Canadian Miss Wellington and her friends gives us an idea of what our refugee women would have had to go through if they had fallen into the hands of the gestapo. She had done nothing against the Nazis but given assistance to refugees.

Miss Warriner also wrote about how they made sure that

their refugee women were not located by the gestapo and then continued:

"Everything seemed to go well. The approximately seventy women were on the train. Miss Margaret Dougan was the traveling guide. The train was due to pull out any minute from Wilson Railway station in Prague. I took leave of the group and was on my way out of the railway station when I saw a group of men rushing through the station out to the train platform. I followed them to the platform where I found the gestapo searching the train. One of the women whispered to me 'They have arrested M.D.'

"I approached the leader of the gestapo troop and said, ' The papers of this woman are in order. She has a British visa and an exit permit from the gestapo, why can she not leave?' He replied, 'The gestapo is not giving any information. This communist mud is traveling under the British flag'.

"In the meantime Margaret Dougan was interrogated and the passports were inspected with remarks about 'the lying and traitorous Englishmen'. The search of the train took on dramatic forms. The doors of the restrooms were forced open. Gestapo officials were running along the train and even looked underneath the train for refugees. The techniques of terror were used to the full extent causing fear for the victims, but in the end were ineffective since the gestapo did not find out in their rush that some of the women had neither passport nor exit permit.

"It was much too easy for the gestapo to check our transports and arrest women they otherwise could not catch. For that reason our British legation in Prague intervened to get passports and exit permits for the women and were successful."

The weight of the British government behind its legation in Prague was the most important factor in getting women refugees out of Prague. Although it still took quite some time, the remaining women were eventually reunited with their loved ones in England and other western European countries.

The experience of those who left Prague on the last special train before the German takeover was described by Alois Mollik in a letter to me:

"It was before eight o'clock in the morning of the day Hitler marched into Prague when Miss Doreen Warriner took

Mrs. Hilda Patz and myself to the British Embassy. When we arrived Wenzel Jaksch, Frank Rehwald and Frank Krejčy were already there in safety. The general secretary of the party, Siegfried Taub, was missing. We got word that he was safe in the Swedish Embassy. Two hours later we learned Mr. Taub was not in the Swedish Embassy but somewhere on the streets. When he was found, Mr. Jaksch asked and got permission from the British Ambassador for Mr. Taub and his wife to stay in the British Embassy.

"In the late afternoon the High Commissioner of the League of Nations drove Mrs. Patz and myself to the Hotel Flora where we stayed the night. We could not stay in the British Embassy because there was no room. Wenceslaus Square, where hundreds of taxicabs usually parked, was empty. The next day a taxicab I had ordered before going to bed, took us to the Polish Embassy where I completed some business. At about three o'clock in the afternoon we boarded a train that took us to the Moravsky Ostrava. After a nine hour delay, caused by technical problems on the train, we continued our journey through Poland to Gdynia."

The four men who had been given refuge in the British Embassy were to wait until British authorities could arrange safe conduct for them. While waiting Wenzel Jaksch thought it would be easier for the others if he left secretly. He decided to try to make it across the Polish border on skis. He succeeded — going over the Beskiden Mountain range into Poland. From there he went to Sweden and then to England. The others waited for safe conduct arrangements to be made and then went to Sweden where Mr. Krejčy took up residence. Mr. Taub later went to the United States where he died in 1946. Mr. Rehwald emigrated to Canada.

By March 15, 1939, when Adolf Hitler took over what was left of Czechoslovakia, our rescue operation had succeeded in getting over 3,000 of the most endangered people out of the country. Many more of our refugees could have been saved if the start of our rescue operation had not been hampered by the problem of our citizenship, and if the promises of visas had been kept. The delays deepened the despair in the camps. Some refugees believed the encouraging letters from relatives and went back to their homes in occupied districts. Many of them were sent to jail or concentration camps when they arrived. They learned too late that the letters were, in many cases, inspired by local Nazi officials. Others, particularly members who lived in Prague or interior cities, believed they were safe. Mrs. Schnabel, one of the volunteers who shared an office with me, was one of these. She did not leave and was caught by the Gestapo. Her friends later learned that she had been murdered in a concentration camp. Dr. Ludwig Czech, former leader of our party and a cabinet minister in the coalition government, believed that he would be safe in his home town of Brno. He was arrested by the Gestapo after the March invasion, and sent to Theresienstadt concentration camp where he was murdered. Dr. Emil Strauss, the editor of our newspaper in Prague, first thought he would be safe in Prague then decided, in February 1939, to emigrate to England. His visa for England came too late, and he was also murdered by the Nazi gestapo. The visa could have saved his life.

Our members and their families who did escape found refuge in Britain, Sweden, Belgium, Denmark, Norway, Finland, and France. Others found refuge and new homes in New Zealand, Australia, the United States, Bolivia and Brazil. With the help of friends our flight to freedom was possible. Their bravery and generosity assisted us in carrying out our emergency escape plan.

4

FLIGHT TO FREEDOM AND EXILE

I left Prague with fifteen other refugees in the early morning of a cold, rainy November day on a commercial flight to Belgium. It had been arranged that after a few days stay in Belgium a freighter would take us by sea to Gotenburg, Sweden, then on by train to Malmoe in the south of Sweden.

The Belgian airplane did not accommodate many more passengers than we sixteen Sudeten German refugees. This was my first experience of air travel. I had a queer feeling in my stomach when the plane was gaining altitude by pushing through the rain laden clouds to fly in the bright sunshine. The strange sensations of flight did not bother me as much as sitting beside an elderly passenger who vomited all the way from Prague to Brussels. His face looked to me as if he would not make it.

What bothered me most was the thought that we had to fly over Nazi Germany. Something could happen that would require us to make an emergency landing, and we would be discovered to be refugees. It had happened. I had heard that planes had been forced to land, and German refugees had fallen into the hands of the Nazi gestapo. During the flight, which took from early morning to about noon, I kept looking for signs of other airplanes. Shortly before we reached the Belgian border, I saw one with swastikas on the fuselage. It was circling our plane. The way I felt my face must have been white as chalk, but I said nothing to my wife nor to members of our group. I just kept watching the Nazi airplane, hopeful that we would reach our destination without trouble.

Soon after this terrifying incident I felt the plane losing altitude. I could see people working in the fields below. The stewardess came by to tell us to buckle our seat belts. When I asked her where we were she said the nicest thing I had heard on the flight: "We are over Belgium and getting ready to land in Brussels". When we stepped on Belgian soil, I could have fallen down on my knees and kissed that still-free earth.

The formalities on landing were soon taken care of. We were driven in an autobus to the office building of a Belgian newspaper, where there was a restaurant. The Refugee Assistance Committee of Brussels had ordered a meal for us, and we received tickets for a train ride to Antwerp. We were to be accommodated in a hostel there until we could leave, in about ten days, for our destination in Sweden. When we arrived in Antwerp we found that the hostel was located in the red light district, not far from the harbor. The seedy atmosphere in the area surrounding our hostel started to get on our shattered nerves but we made ourselves as comfortable as possible in these surroundings. Our sleep was disturbed by the regular fights of competing prostitutes. They fought in doorways or in the streets by pulling hair and screaming obscenities. We, fortunately, could only understand the tone.

Our stay in Antwerp was short. The days of waiting for the freighter loading its cargo of long steel beams seemed to us like weeks. The only bright and cheering moments we had were when we went to Mother Marie's restaurant, around the corner from our hostel. Our meals were paid for by the local refugee assistance committee. Mother Marie never failed to cheer us up with stories which she told us in pretty good German. She was known to many sailors from Liverpool to Singapore, and she sure had some amusing stories to tell about her acquaintances. The way she mothered us and encouraged us to eat her delicious meals, I don't think she made one franc of profit out of catering to us. Bless her good soul. We were her daily guests until the last week of November, 1938, when the freighter, taking us along as passengers, pulled up its anchor and started down the wide River Scheldt, toward the North Sea and our destination in Sweden.

Our accommodation on the freighter was by no means of Queen Mary standards. But who cared in our situation. We were beggars then. We realized that the choice was not ours. The women and children of our group were assigned to cabins midships, above the main deck. The only man given a cabin with his wife was a former journalist from Teplitz, Frank Seidel, who was not feeling well when we boarded the ship. The other men, Rudolf Geissler, Karl Iser, Fritz Hopf, Max Heinrich, and myself, were assigned to a former crew cabin. In order to get to our cabin we had to climb down a steel ladder from 'midship, to the top of the steel cargo, go across to another steel ladder and up to the aft deck, then down again to our cabin. One elderly member of the crew was assigned to look after us. He brought our luggage to us and straightened up the wooden double bunks on which we were to sleep.

As soon as the heavily loaded freighter hit the open sea, it started raining. The rain came down like a flood. Driven by the wind, the storm reached a crescendo causing the freighter to roll, and with it the stomachs of most of my mates began to roll. I was not affected. Fritz Hopf hailed from Karlsbad in Western Bohemia, where they made a brand of liquor which was supposed to be an effective remedy for stomach trouble. He brought out a bottle he had carried with him and was passing it around for a swig when our Swedish attendant stepped into our cabin. Our friend offered his bottle to our guest, who recognized the contents at once. He said, in broken German and Swedish, "That's good for the moga" — meaning stomach. It sure must have done his "moga" lots of good, for he returned several times until the bottle was empty. I did not see any effect the drink had on my friends' sea sickness; they continued rushing up to the railings on deck to feed the fish.

I was the only one among us who did not get seasick. I felt like going to have breakfast the next morning. When I came up on the deck of the rolling ship, one wave after another was washing across the cargo and off the other side. After running across the deck between waves, I reached the dining room. When I entered the Captain was the only person there. He told me that the storm had been so bad during the night that some waves had come up as high as the upper deck. Water had even run into the dining room. He also told me that the wind strength had reached eleven. To my question as to what that meant, he answered that just one more point would have meant that SOS signals would have been sent.

During the day the storm calmed down a little. Some of my friends began to recover from their sea sickness.

By the next morning our experience with the raging sea was over. After three days on a rolling ship it took a while to get used to walking on solid ground again. Once again, in Gotenburg, on solid ground, even the ones who suffered most from sea sickness came back to normal.

We went to the station restaurant. As we sat at our tables, no one seemed in a hurry to order. We studied the menu like a cat would study a calendar. The menu was all in Swedish, which none of us could read. "Well", said one of my companions, "why don't you order? You have a pocket dictionary, look it up." I tried but could find nothing. A waitress, who must have heard us talking German, came over to our table and asked in German what we would like to eat. She translated the menu for us. I, still holding my pocket dictionary in my hand, felt like a fool. We all ordered and enjoyed our meal. We laughed about each other's ignorance of the language of the country of our asylum.

The train to Malmoe was due to leave Gotenburg late in the afternoon. We had lots of time for a stroll through parts of that strange and beautiful city. The train trip to Malmoe was uneventful. At that time of year it gets dark early in the northern countries and we did not see much. It was close to midnight when we arrived in Malmoe on December 1, 1938. Some members of the local refugee assistance committee were waiting at the railway station. One of the members of this welcoming committee gave us necessary instructions in our own language. We listened very carefully to what this Swedish friend had to say. We were taken to a hotel where we were to stay until other accommodation could be made available for us. Every family was assigned a room of their own. The rooms were nice and inviting. Our first night of sleep in peace. Our apprehension about the future was no deterrant to a good night of sleep after our hectic journey.

Next morning we were called for breakfast. The tables were loaded with a variety of Swedish dishes, some of them strange to us, but good tasting. It was the first time in my life that I had sat down at such a nicely arranged table in a hotel dining room without having to pay for the food before me. That first meal in Sweden and the meals to follow were no great pleasure for me. I believe my companions felt the same way. As tasty as the food was, it was food we had not earned by working. It was provided by people who had worked and earned the money for it, but were filled with charity and sympathy for us in our plight. The feelings about our future nagged us. Would we live in an apartment or some refugee camp? Would we be able to find employment in Sweden? Could we earn our own food and shelter and become independent of charity again? These and other questions in our minds prevented us from feeling cheerful or having an optimistic outlook.

We, who went to Malmoe, did not have to live in mass refugee quarters. We were moved into apartments about a week before Christmas. The public welfare organization of Malmoe donated furniture so we could furnish our apartments. When we moved into our apartment I should have felt very happy and privileged: I did not. I was thinking about the many refugees who still waited in some refugee camp in Czechoslovakia. About those, in other countries, who were not as lucky as we.

The rent for my assigned apartment was eighty Swedish kronor per month with some of the utilities extra. The apartment consisted of a kitchen, bathroom and two bedrooms. I leased one of these bedrooms to a refugee from Austria. Mr. Freitag was single and a double refugee. He had to flee from Austria, in February 1934, when the fascist Dollfuss regime came to power. He had gone to live in Teplitz in the Sudetenland until he had to flee again, with us, after the Munich debacle. Freitag paid thirty kronor for his room and the use of the kitchen and bath. The arrangement was of mutual advantage, as both of us saved some money.

We received 150 kronor assistance from the Malmoe Refugee Relief Committee, which was financed by the trade unions, the Social Democratic Party and public collections. The last day of every month we had to go to the office of the Committee to pick up our money. Never before in my life had I collected money I had not earned by my work. That was my pride all my life. Oh, how I hated those monthly walks to that office! I hated it even though I knew that this money was given to us not out of pure pity but as an act of international solidarity.

The change from the hotel room to the apartment aroused some new hope in me: everything would work out all right for us eventually. The arrangement with Freitag gave me a ray of hope; after payment of the rent, the one hundred kronor left could be stretched a little in order to pay for living expenses. We could also save a few kroner for material to fix up our furniture. That prospect alone, just thinking about it and planning it, put some creative thoughts back into my mind.

I had plenty of time on my hands to make the repairs if I could get some tools. As a cabinetmaker's son, I felt that some skill may have rubbed off from my father who I remembered as very skillful in his trade. Our landlord, a stout, good-hearted Swede, offered me his workshop and tools in the basement of the apartment. When the next assistance payment came we had succeeded in saving a few kronor, so I bought some materials and went to work.

Just after we were moved into apartments, we received an invitation to a Christmas celebration from the Malmoe Refugee Assistance Committee. It was a fine gesture by our hosts. Thinking back now, after so many years have passed, it becomes clear to me that none of us were in high spirits nor pictures of joyfulness that evening.

Our mood lifted when two familiar faces came through the door. The first was Ernst Paul, who had come from Prague to visit his wife. Mrs. Paul was living as a refugee in Sweden. Ernst had stayed in Prague to continue his work with the refugee rescue operation. The second was Axel Granath, secretary of the Swedish refugee assistance organization, and an acquaintance from Prague. He had an accordian slung over his shoulder and later played for us. The appearance of these two good friends and protectors was a great surprise. Ernst Paul gave a short report about the situation in Prague. Difficulties still troubled the efforts of our party in getting our refugees out of the country to safety. We sat there in safety in a free country which did its best to make us feel at home. We realized that we should feel grateful: We did. Still, the nagging thoughts about our friends in some poorly organized refugee camp in Czechoslovakia made lumps come to our throats. We realized our luck in having been assigned to the first few small groups flown to Sweden and England.

After a delicious dinner, Axel Granath played some snappy Swedish tunes on his accordian and sang some lovely folk songs. We enjoyed the music, but we did not understand the words. Then he asked us to sing some Christmas songs in German. We sang a number of them. I remember how I choked and how tears started to run down my cheeks when we started to sing "Stille nacht, Heilige nacht" — Silent night, holy night. Never before had I felt as sentimental at Christmas as I did that night as a political refugee in Sweden. It seemed as though the ground under my feet had disappeared and my eyes looked into a future which did not exist. We did not know whether we would be fugitives and beggars for the rest of our lives or whether we would find employment and a livelihood in this country where we had found refuge from Nazi persecution.

After Christmas besides working on my furniture, I was kept busy trying to learn the Swedish language in order to go job hunting. It would probably have been somewhat easier to find a job if I had been a tradesman, but I was a political secretary with some experience in a number of industrial jobs. My best chance I thought would be in the textile industry. Before my political appointments, I had gained some skill in that type of work. A textile worker, Edmund Franz, lived in the same apartment building as I did. He could speak German because his wife was a native of Luebeck. When I got acquainted with him through our friendly landlord, he promised to talk to his employer about a job for me. His employer was a Jew who miraculously was able to still sell his products in Germany. My friend did all right until he told his employer that I was a political refugee from the Sudetenland. He told me that his employer said that he could not hire me because he would lose his exports to Germany. He explained to my friend that there were so many Nazi spies in Malmoe that he would be ruined if they found out that he had hired me.

Some of my companion refugees, with trade skills, found work while I still had to go every month on those hated walks to pick up my assistance. I lost hope of finding a job. Thus when the first opportunity to emigrate came along, I applied to go to Canada. I was accepted. My friends in Malmoe tried to convince me that, with a little more patience, I would finally find a job. That would have been true, since all of my friends got jobs when war broke out and Sweden was in need of workers. I had made up my mind, however. One of my dearest friends, who had high regard for me and could not picture me going into the uncertainty of pioneer farming in Canada (for which I had no experience whatsoever), tried several times to talk me out of it. He failed.

At the end of June 1939, we went to Stockholm where a commission of the Canadian Immigration Department gave us medical examinations and the admission documents for Canada. About two weeks later, on July 11, we boarded a Finnish ship sailing to Hull, England. The next day we boarded the Montrose, in Liverpool. On the evening of the same day, we were with a group of other refugees from Sweden and England on our way to Canada, our new homeland.

5

EMIGRATION

While the first refugees sent out of Czechoslovakia were learning new languages and looking for work in other countries, the work of the party-organized rescue continued in Prague. Our envoys in London continued to seek financial aid and countries willing to accept large numbers of refugees. Those remaining in refugee camps became more desperate as they waited for interim passports, visas and transportation arrangements. The individuals who had voluntarily gone to Prague continued to assist the rescue operation. Miss Doreen Warriner, who did so much to help us, wrote the following letter to the **Manchester Guardian**, in December, 1938.

"I shall direct your attention to the urgency of the situation here for the refugees. The real tragedy is the situation of the Sudeten German Social Democrats. There are about 4,000 of them. They have been starving during the past eight weeks. Nobody cared for them, and they are desperate and have lost hope for better conditions. Since the decision about the right of option, no prospect exists for them to find work in Czechoslovakia. At the present there are no Sudeten Germans in the camps who can return to Germany without endangering their lives. They are now starting to ask whether despite that, they should return.

"The present measures of direct help to the camps, from the Lord Mayor of London fund, is insufficient. All the camps I have seen are overcrowded, few have coal and a number of people are suffering from a lack of nourishment. The only means to help these people would be if the possibility of group emigration could be made available. Every other measure to help these people is only soothing our own conscience. In the past few days I have received offers of cigarettes and chocolates for Christmas, which proves that, in Great Britain, no clear conception exists of the real situation.

"These people have, during the past five years, fought a hopeless battle against Nazism. In the crisis and in spite of all dangers, they stood faithful to their principles. In the last two months they have suffered because nobody did anything for them. They are exposed to all kinds of small measures of persecution, which in the work camps are increasing. They have lost all hope for a future. All these circumstances indicate that the refugees are in a peculiar situation, and the present measure for their emigration to England must be reviewed.

"Firstly, it is absolutely necessary to change the existing regulations for granting visas. People who are coming to me to apply for visas are mostly middle class people who believe that by claiming their influential connections they could go to England more easily. Yet, the people in the camps have no such connections. The only possibility to organize their emigration in a just and practical manner, would be granting of group visas for a certain number, then sending representatives from the Dominions to select suitable people for employment. Organization by individual persons or welfare organizations unavoidably leads to patronizing. Secondly, sources of finances for settlement in countries overseas will be needed. It would be approximately 2,000 families, which should not be too big a problem.

"When the right form of organization is found and the financial means provided the problem should be solved easily. Seen from the standpoint of the labor market, these people are highly qualified and the representatives of the Dominions are very well informed as to what their needs are. If a decision is not made soon, a chance will be missed."

This appeal, for some organized, practical, government sponsored means of getting the remaining Sudeten German refugees out of Czechoslovakia, came at about the same time as British politicians were questioning the use of a reconstruction loan granted to the Czech government. The loan of ten million pounds, approximately forty-five million dollars, had been negotiated in October. The representatives of the Czech government, Messrs. Pospišil, Peroutka and Målik, had publicly stated that: "In the use of this loan there will be no discrimination for racial or political reasons." There was not, however, any clear indication of how the loan had been used by November.

Sir George Harvey, a Conservative member of the British parliament, in a speech on November 8, 1939, made it clear what was expected in the use of the loan in Czechoslovakia. He said: "A nation which has lost one third of its territory and one third of its population, perhaps sacrificed more of its economic wealth to prevent a European war, has done nobly. Thus we should recognize our debt and obligation to the people of Czechoslovakia, in fact not only to those who can remain in their country but also to those from the Sudeten districts who have left their old homeland. Many of them cannot stay in the remaining districts of Czechoslovakia and are looking for other places to stay in other lands. I hope that measures will be taken so that a considerable portion of that money will be used for assistance in the emigration plans of the dislodged people.

"I believe that the government has already tried to use her good offices to encourage the Dominions to open their doors for these refugees from the Sudetenland. I hope that all in its power will be done to get places for settlement in the crown colonies....We owe these people a great debt. I hope the government will realize that in its endeavors to help them they will have public opinion in the country behind it."

Soon after this speech, the British government replaced the voluntary organizations helping the refugees with the semi-public Czech Refugee Trust Fund. The fund was the responsibility of the Home Office.

While the British government was making this decision, Sudeten German representatives in London were in contact with Canadian officials. Two representatives, Frank Rehwald and Willi Wanka, were sent to Canada to negotiate directly with the Canadian Immigration Department. The simultaneous negotiations in London and Ottawa resulted in Canada agreeing to accept 300 families and a number of single men. The conditions for admission to Canada were that an amount of $1500 per family and $900 per single man be deposited into the settlement funds of two Canadian railway companies and that all transportation costs be paid by the immigrants. The immigrants were to be settled on land controlled by the Canadian Pacific Railway Company and the Canadian National Railway Company. Each company was to be responsible for approximately half of those admitted. The representatives of the Sudeten Germans were to be responsible for advising their people of these conditions, and of the choice of location offered — individual abandoned farms in northern Saskatchewan or a communal settlement in the virgin bushland of British Columbia.

It is an understatement to say that the financial problems of the Sudeten German refugees seemed hopeless when faced with the need to finance our own emigration. Without a large amount of money, not a single settler could be sent to Canada. Since none of the refugees had money, the money had to be raised. The British government decision to establish the Czech Refugee Trust Fund enabled our London representatives to obtain funds to pay for our transportation and make the deposit with the railway companies.

With the financial problem of emigration to Canada solved, it was certain that the Canadian Immigration Department would send a commission to Europe to examine applicants and provide them with the necessary documents. Willi Wanka and his wife Mitzi worked in close liaison with Canadian immigration officials. They made sure that every applicant was notified when and where medical examinations for prospective settlers were to be held. They compiled lists of accepted applicants and their choice of location for transportation arrangements. Putting these lists together was not an easy task; many wives and children of accepted applicants were still in refugee camps in Czechoslovakia and had to be brought to England. No married man could leave England, or in fact any other country, without having all members of his family reunited before departure for Canada. Then there was the problem of whether a family preferred to go to their own farm or to a communal settlement. In listing these preferences, Mr. Wanka and his assistants always had to keep in mind the necessity of equally dividing the applicants between the settlements.

Since most of our refugees wanting to settle in Canada lived in England, the Immigration Department officials started their work there and took several weeks to examine applicants.

Not all applicants were accepted. Some were rejected because they did not meet the health standards; others because they were considered too old for such a venture. In selecting the settlers, the commission did an excellent job for the railway companies: The oldest married man accepted was fifty-four, the youngest twenty; the oldest single man accepted was fifty-one, the youngest seventeen. Of the 1024 persons who came to Canada, 387 were under twenty-two years of age. The youngest child was only six weeks old.

In spite of the difficulties and disappointments encountered in organizing our emigration, the operation proceeded swiftly. The first twenty-five families, and a number of single men, left Southampton on April 8, 1939 aboard the Montcalm. From then until July 28, at approximately two week intervals, the refugees left the ports of Southampton and Liverpool aboard ships owned by the Canadian railway companies. Our emigration was good business for these companies at a time when the depression was just bottoming out.

Of the 305 families and single men who went to Canada, the majority, 224 families, left temporary refuge in England. The remainder came from Belgium, Denmark, France, Sweden, Finland and Norway. Three families, who were not members of the land settlement group, went to Prescott, Ontario, to work as glovemakers. One hundred and fifty families and thirty-five single men traveled to northern Saskatchewan while one hundred and fifty-two families and thirty-seven single men settled in north eastern British Columbia.

Thanks to the help we received from our friends and the British government we were able to accept the Canadian immigration offer. We can say with pride that the Sudeten German settlers did not cost Canada a single cent. The only thanks the Sudeten German settlers owe to Canada is for opening the door for us so we would not fall victim to Nazi persecution. We appreciate that and have done our utmost to be useful to the country.

6

FEARS AND FIRST IMPRESSIONS

The fears and nagging thoughts which troubled us as political refugees in exile continued as we sailed across the Atlantic to our new homeland. Urban people with no experience in farming did not fit well into Canadian immigration policy, which favored farmers. Most of us were skilled industrial workers, tradesmen or white-collar workers of all kinds. There were former members of parliament, newspapermen, teachers, doctors, political party or trade union organizers, but no farmers. Would we be able to farm? How did a man farm? Was the land productive? Where exactly were we going? The feeling of relief on being accepted as immigrants to Canada and the activities of preparing for the journey had pushed these doubts out of our minds. Aboard ship these doubts returned. We were no longer political refugees seeking asylum, but we were not farmers either.

Traveling by train from Montreal to the Peace River district of British Columbia gave us the first hint of the vastness of our new homeland. As I traveled through the prairie provinces in July, 1939, I was aware of this vastness but I recall more vividly the many ugly sights. The windows of farmsteads were gaping holes bordered by broken glass. Doors were torn off, or still flapping in the wind. Fences were broken, the posts still hanging on wires or nails, and partly covered with sand or topsoil. Weeds were growing in the farm yards and around the houses. These were sights I will never forget for the rest of my life. I had known that Canada had also experienced the depression but did not know the effects.

The sight of these abandoned farms filled my traveling

companions and I with fears; perhaps some similar depressing area might have been selected for our settlement. Having come from a densely populated, developed country, we had no idea what it would be like to live in primitive conditions such as we were now seeing. I remember discussing with one of my traveling companions the dreary sights we had seen. It still makes me smile when I recall his main concern. When he saw the many shaky outhouses leaning in the wind or lying near the abandoned houses, he realized that we would need baths and would have no bath tub or indoor plumbing facilities. We would have to brave the elements like those farmers had to do. Since my friend had left a well-paying white collar job and a modern furnished apartment in Prague, the thought of outhouses was very depressing to him. By chance this man later became my neighbor, but by that time he had become seasoned to the outhouses and the tin wash tubs.

None of our group could speak either of the languages of Canada when we arrived. Our contact with the people of our new homeland was limited to immigration or railway company officials until we arrived in Winnipeg. It was very refreshing to be welcomed in our own language by a gentleman who came into our coach to hand us some gifts. That fine Canadian was John Devigneux, who had come to Canada from Germany many years before. We had heard about him from members of our group who had passed through Winnipeg before. Devigneux did not miss a single one of the trains carrying Sudeten German refugees. He always went to the railway station to welcome each group and offer his help and advice. The friendly, familiar words of this man remained in our memories as a nice introduction to Canada. A word of welcome or encouragement and the offer of advice or assistance was always a pleasant experience for political refugees.

The first group of Sudeten German settlers who had left England on April 8, 1939, arrived at the Tupper Creek railway station in British Columbia on April 22, 1939.
Their names were:

Anton Augsten & family
Alfred David & family
Arnold Brumlik & family

Valentin Dittrich & family
Alois Mueller & family
Rudolf Mader & family
Josef Nodes & family
Hubert Leinsmer & family
Heinrich Mazanek & family
Franz Reilich & family
Fridolin Reinelt & family
William Haeckl & family
Ernest Kreuzer & family
Herman Seidel & family
Karl Seidel & family
Max Otto Siegert & family
Franz Suttner & family
Grete Loew
Henry Weisbach & family
Herbert Wiesner & family
Franz Tamm & family
Josef Tillner & family
Nicu Sommert & family
Josef Linay
Anton Watzl & family
Frank Zapf & family

The group's first sight of the settlement, which was to be their new home, was the shack called a railway station and a few houses. Because the houses were not ready the travelers had to stay one more night in their railway cars. The next day sixteen families were moved into eight log houses. The remaining nine families had to stay in the railway station. The men swore and the women wept in disappointment. The disappointment deepened when only half a can of milk was given to them for their children; barely enough to wet their tongues.

The log houses had no rainproofing on the roof. The wind whistled through the walls, since only a few had had moss pressed into the cracks. With the help of the sixteen families already in houses, a few more cabins were thrown together. The nine families who had stayed in the railway station were moved into their unfinished cabins the third day after they arrived. Everyone squeezed together like sardines to get some sleep on the floors of their overcrowded shelters.

One man did not feel like leaving the railway car at all when the remaining families were assigned to more unfinished log houses. His companions nicknamed him "the railway farmer" and he had to endure lots of kidding about that later.

As these families were moved, they received one empty sack for two persons in each family to make a straw mattress. The straw could be obtained from a pile in the old ranch yard nearby. There were no bedsteads, thus everyone had to bed himself down on the floor. Every family also received: one bag of flour, twenty-five pounds of rice, one bag of oatmeal, ten pounds of lard, twenty-five pounds of dry prunes, half a bag of potatoes, half a bag of carrots, one bag of grits, ten pounds of syrup, one dozen eggs, twenty pounds of dry beans, one tin of marmalade, and some salt, pepper, and other spices. Meat remained just a dream for many weeks, unless one was lucky enough to kill a prairie chicken or rabbit with a rock or piece of wood. None of the settlers had a hunting gun to go after a moose or deer.

Every man received an axe; every two men a hammer and a hand saw; every four men one bow saw; every eight men a long pull saw for cutting logs and firewood. Nails were made available from the supplies for building houses. Kitchen utensils had been stored in one of the log houses along with the food items. A member of the supervisory staff of the Canadian Colonization Association told the settlers to take the utensils they needed. Naturally everyone ran to the storeroom. The ones who came last had to leave empty-handed for there were not enough. Some people had taken more items than they were supposed to receive. Without utensils it was almost impossible for the women to prepare meals. The women also wanted washboards for their laundry. None were available and they were told: "What do you need a washboard for? A washboard wears out your laundry."

After a number of days had gone by, some lumber was made available to every household for building furniture. First of all, a primitive bedstead was built to get the straw mattress off the cold floor. Some of the families learned that when a barrel of nails was emptied it could be used as a stool. They lived in "comfort" while others watched like hawks for the next barrel. Others nailed together pieces of rough lumber left over from building bedsteads and tables to form a sort of stool.

Each family was supplied with one pail. This pail had to be used to carry water from the creek for household needs; it served as a container for waste water, and it was used as a milk pail. In short, it served every purpose a pail could be made to serve. No lamps were available to light the houses. It got dark early in the evening and the only light was obtained by opening the door of the wood-burning kitchen stove. This gave some light mixed with smoke when the wind caused a down draft in the stove pipe chimney. Finally a carton of lamps was found behind one of the log buildings. The lamps were distributed to the settlers but there was no kerosene for them. That meant some more swearing by the men and tears from the women. The settlers were becoming inventive; their needs were strong. If there was no kerosene for the lamps, why not use the caterpillar tractor oil supplies. This oil was used in the lamps. It gave some light, but also an evil odor which filled the houses.

The weather conditions in northern British Columbia, in April, were very different than that in our former homeland. Spring came much earlier in Czechoslovakia and by April a large part of the spring work was done on the farms. In the Peace River country, however, some snow was still on the ground, and the nights were cold. Living in unfinished houses was very unpleasant when melting snow and rain ran through the roof. Shortly after the first group had arrived, there was a heavy rain storm. The rain soaked everything in the houses. A bag of flour just needed some salt and it could have been kneaded into dough for bread. Some neighboring homesteaders told the newcomers to protect themselves from future rain storms by nailing black insulation paper on the roof. That was a help, until a strong wind came up and made the paper fly all over the country because there was no lumber to hold it down.

The group had heard tales of timber wolves, bears, cougars, and coyotes, which caused apprehension for some. The first arrivals saw few of these animals, but the odd moose and several jack rabbits were around the settlement in the early spring. The moose and coyote were strange as were some of the birds. People were surprised by the tameness of the grouse, known as a prairie chicken. These birds soon learned to hurry away from the settlers, because many landed in the frying pan of those who hunted the birds with a stick or a rock. The sounds of coyotes howling was strange, but very seldom did anyone see one of these shy creatures at close range.

The strange surroundings, the inadequate housing, and frustration over spoiled food supplies and utensil shortages caused a great deal of dissatisfaction and arguments among the settlers. In order to straighten things out, the settlers elected a three-man committee, Valentin Dittrich, Henry Weisbach, and Josef Tillner. These men were to present the settlers' problems to the settlement administration. Valentin Dittrich and Henry Weisbach collected some of the utensils so each family could cook meals. The committee also requested another pail for each family. After several weeks of haggling with the settlement manager, the pails arrived.

The first arrivals were very busy as they had to help build houses for the settlers coming later and start to clear the land. The tools they had received were used to help the native building crew build frame houses, eighteen by fourteen feet in size, for the people scheduled to arrive on May 19. Since not every man had been issued a hammer and saw, some were assigned to clear land and cut grasses for hay. The women in the group were assigned a plot of cleared land to grow a vegetable garden. There were many mix-ups in distribution of work assignments and supplies for the first groups to arrive. In order to stem the growing dissatisfaction among the settlers, the supervisors set up a department system with members of the settlers' committee and a few others in charge of each department. Alois Mueller and Henry Weisbach were designated to get some organization into the haphazard work arrangements. Josef Tillner became a sort of supply chief for milk and water. Valentin Dittrich was assigned to look after the food and other needs of the families. This arrangement helped to speed up the work and overcome some of the problems.

These were the conditions when I arrived at Tupper station, on July 25, 1939. There were no houses ready for us because there had not been enough hands to handle the urgent work of landclearing, haying, gardening, and house building. It had become standard procedure for new arrivals to have to spend one more night in the railway coaches, and so it was with our group. We arrived on Tuesday and were told we would have to wait until the next day to be taken to settlement headquarters. When we arrived there, we were issued a small tent for each family and a large gunny sack to be filled with straw for a mattress. Like others before me, I went to the straw pile to fill the sack. On my way there I spotted a pile of lumber and asked one of the already established settlers, who functioned as some kind of foreman, if I could take some boards to make a bedstead. He said that I could, and after filling my sack with straw and carrying it back to the tent, I borrowed some tools from a settler, picked up some boards, and went to work.

While I was busy building the bedstead, Alois Mueller came to our tent carrying some queer looking tools over his shoulder. These turned out to be three scythes, one of which he leaned against our tent and the other two at tents nearby. After he had deposited the other scythes, he came back to tell me that early next morning I had to go west to cut grass for hay. He told me the names of my haymaking companions and that we would have to start very early next morning. When he left I went back to work on our bedstead.

That night when we finally settled down for our first night in the tent, we soon realized there was not much hope of getting any sleep. Mosquitoes had moved into the tent with us. We were fresh blood for them and they sure enjoyed us to their hearts' content, humming around our eyes and ears, then crawling under our blankets to fill their bellies with our blood.

I was afraid of horses, but did not have to deal with this fear when I first arrived. I did have to learn to use that queer looking tool, the scythe, and to use muscles unused by a district secretary of a political party. The mosquitoes also made me uncomfortable.

The settlers learned later that they had made an impression on the Canadian people in cities where the train had stopped. The following is an excerpt from an article in the **Edmonton Journal** of April 21, 1939, describing the arrival of the first Sudeten German settlers. The headline read: "Refugees from Sudeten Welcome Here. 25 Families Go Through City en Route to North. Will try farming."

"Eagerly facing a new life in a country they know is free, 25 families—refugees who fled from Sudeten German territory a few hours before Hitler's battalions arrived—passed through Edmonton Thursday afternoon on their way to occupy 30,000 acres of farm land at Tupper Creek, 450 miles north of Edmonton in the Peace River district.

"There were 87 in all, many of them children. Few have had any experience at farming, coming as they did from industrial areas of Reichenberg and Gablonz, but they have no fears about building themselves a new and happy and spacious existence on the land.

"The party traveled in two private day coaches, which were switched from the incoming C.P.R. train to the C.N.R. depot where they were attached to the N.A.R. train going to the north.

"There were few solemn faces among the group. Little children ran up and down the C.N.R. platform as their parents waited for the train to leave and just like Canadian children or children anywhere in the world for that matter, they got into their little troubles, such as getting in the way of the 'platform mules', those small motored trucks which haul baggage trucks around.

"Teenage girls walked arm and arm up and down the platform and giggled on occasion. Some looked toward the city."

"One could almost see the surprise on the face of a mother as a C.N.R. constable reached down and patted the head of a little boy perhaps three years old. The child looked up quizzically. The constable, mother and child smiled and the incident was over.

"Those who remember the 'immigrant trains' of other years said that the newcomers appeared 'different' from those who came before. Whereas the immigrant trains brought women with colorful shawls about their heads, and men wearing typical European dress, these people looked 'like some of us' as one observer put it. Most of them were dressed neatly.

"They were strangers in a strange land as they left for the north but most of them looked as if they could 'make a go of it.'

"Accompanying them was Paul Cook, representative of the Canada Colonization Association at Winnipeg, and the party was met here by C. A. Buchanan, district supervisor of the association at Edmonton. They arrived at St. John on the liner Montcalm and travelled across Canada by C.P.R., arriving here at 3:35 p.m. Thursday and leaving by N.A.R. at 5:40 p.m.

"About 60 Czech and Slovak residents of the city, among them Jean and Milo Zima,...both of whom fled from Czechoslovakia just before the September crisis, gathered at the C.N.R. station to give the party a cheerful send-off on the last 450 mile stretch of their long journey.

"About 100 baskets of foodstuff prepared in the kitchens of Czech homes in Edmonton—all of them containing goodly supplies of the favorite national food of Czecho-Slovakia, poppy seed cake—were piled on the train before it pulled out. Many city merchants had given milk, bread and fruit to be given to the party as well.

"Edmonton gave the party its most welcome surprise since it came to Canada, declared refugees, some of whom were weeping tears of joy at this reception, and at the breath of native air it brought them 5,000 miles from home. Children ran wild, excited at hearing their tongue spoken by strangers.

"As the train finally pulled out of the station, taking them on the last leg of their long and not always happy journey, members of the party were looking from the windows, their faces beaming with smiles, broader than they have been scarcely any time since their homeland was taken from them."

Despite the many problems, disappointments, and frustrations of becoming established in the settlement, our worst fears did not come true. The surroundings were somewhat similar to the Sudetenland but the weather was colder. No one was threatened by the wild animals. The land was not dry and windswept, but covered with trees and brush. Our houses were somewhat better than those we had seen from the train and we began to realize the harsh realities of our new lives as pioneer farmers.

7

THE LAND SETTLEMENT COMPANY

The Canadian Pacific Railway Company had been granted twenty-five million acres of land on the prairies by the federal government when it undertook construction of the first transcontinental rail line. Other railway companies were also granted land when branch lines and other transcontinental links were built. As a result of these grants the railway companies created special branches within their mangement structures for the purpose of utilizing land holdings. The Canadian Colonization Association was the settlement branch of the Canadian Pacific Railway, given the task of disposing of the company's land. For several years before our group emigrated, the Canadian Colonization Association had promoted settlement, sold land, and transported thousands of experienced European farmers to Western Canada. These operations were assisted by the Canadian government's immigration policy favoring farmers. By 1939, when our group was accepted as immigrants to Canada, the emigration policy was the same and the Association was experienced in assisting farm settlements, and it was given the responsibility of settling our group.

Our settlement was one of the first experiments in settling non-farmers on farms. To my knowledge there has not since been an experiment of this type and magnitude. No other urban, political refugees have been settled under the same conditions. Our people wanted to be settled close together and for that purpose the Association purchased privately owned land. That land was known as the Tate Creek Ranch, in the Peace River district of British Columbia. Over a period of three years additional land was purchased from the British Columbia government and from several individual landholders. The total area of the settlement was 23,628 acres, of which it was estimated that about 15,000 acres was tillable.

Our representatives, who had negotiated the emigration, had not seen the area which eventually became our home. Until we arrived, all we knew of it was that it included a ranch of 16,000 acres, of which 650 acres were cultivated, and that the two nearest towns would be thirteen and twenty miles away. As it turned out the land was slightly rolling similar to the Sudentenland, covered with trees, and interpersed with streams, sloughs and muskeg.

The Czech Refugee Trust Fund, which had been set up in Britain, had deposited $260,000 with the Canada Colonization Association to cover the cost of settling the group. Supervision of the settlement was to begin in March 1939. An account was set up for each family and single man, with a credit of $1,500 and $900 respectively. It has been agreed that $17,050 out of the Fund would be set aside for supervisory expenses. The first deductions from the settlers accounts were for this purpose—one hundred dollars per family and fifty dollars per single man. The cost of food supplies, tools, lumber, farm equipment, and livestock were to be charged to individual accounts when these items were distributed.

A general store was set up and food supplies, tools, and clothing were distributed from there. A holding company, known as the Tate Creek Development Company, was formed to serve as the purchasing and holding agent for land, livestock, and equipment. Bulk purchase of food, some lumber and tools were handled by the company, then items were distributed and charged to settlers accounts. The supervisors of the settlement managed the holding company, while the board of directors were all C.P.R. officials. A blacksmith shop and butcher shop were also set up to provide for the needs of the settlers.

The supervisory staff consisted of Chief Supervisor, Mr. F. B. McConnell, several assistant supervisors including Mr. A. W. McArton, Mr. Bowman, Mr. Sawatsky, and an accountant, Mr. Cook. Bowman and Cook both spoke German. A local blacksmith operated the forge; a settler operated the butcher shop. By 1940 it was recognized by the settlers and management that the land purchased was not prime agricultural land and that actual productive land was much less than the estimated 15,000 acres. A plan was worked out to allow members of the group who did not want to farm or who were, in the opinion of the supervisors, unable to farm, to leave the settlement. The Association helped these people find suitable employment. When a settler left the settlement for a permanent job he gave up his claim to settlement funds and returned his livestock, equipment and land to the Tate Creek Development Company. Settlers who left under these conditions had their railway ticket and moving expenses paid out of the settlement fund. Fifty-nine families and twelve single ment left the settlement before 1943.

Within the settlement, settlers were first settled in small groups at various locations on the Tate Creek Ranch property. These groups usually contained fifteen to twenty households. A large communal barn accommodated livestock cared for by the group.

It was our understanding that, in return for the funds deposited with the Canada Colonization Association, we would receive a minimum of one quarter section of land, of which twenty acres would be broken for crop production. Besides that, we were promised a frame or log house, the essential outfittings required for a start in farming, as well as an amount of money every month for our maintenance until we reached the stage of earning income from our farms.

We were disappointed at a settlement meeting held during the winter of 1939/40, when the supervisor declared that we would not all receive the promised outfits for farming and would not be given title to our land right away. At this meeting Mr. McConnell promised that in the spring of 1940, about forty families would be moved to their quarter sections of land and be outfitted with the following: three cows, one pregnant sow, one horse, for each family; one two-shared plow or horse drawn binder, one wagon, and one sleigh for two families. Mr. McConnell then promised that, for every one of these families, twenty acres of their land would be broken as soon as it was cleared so they could have their own crops next year. The families to be moved were to be located in such a way that each family would have their house on their own land, but at the same time be able to work together building barns, clearing land, have the use of two teams of horses, and have the use of more machinery.

The settlers, because of their disappointment, demanded to get established on a piece of land of their own and get outfitted with the promised livestock and equipment. These demands became louder and louder until it became evident that a rush to the land had started. Before even the first houses were moved, the number of settlers wanting to get moved swelled to seventy-five.

In May 1942, land contracts were made out for the purchase of the land we had been assigned. The contracts were between the Tate Creek Development Company Limited and individual settlers. Appendix #11 is a sample of the land contracts. We were surprised to read in the contract that the land had to be developed and the livestock properly cared for or it could be taken away again.

The Tate Creek Development Company was controlled by the representatives of the railway company until January 12, 1943, when the settlers took over. In January 1942, two settlers were appointed as directors of the company and a third settler was appointed in June. During the last three months of 1942, applications for one share each were taken from all who had signed land contracts. The shares were valued at ten dollars, and could be purchased with a downpayment of fifty cents. On December 26, 1942, the settler shareholders selected a board of eight directors, who were formally elected at a meeting of the company on January 12, 1943. The settlers took over complete control of the Tate Creek Development Company and the management of the Canada Colonization Association ended.

Appendix III represents statements taken from a 1955 progress report by the Canada Colonization Association mailed to all settlers still in possession of their land. These figures show not only the progress of the Sudeten German farming community over sixteen years but the quick improvement made by the settlers in the first four years.

It should be pointed out that not all the livestock, equipment, or machinery were purchased by the settlement company. For example, one hundred and seven horses had been distributed among the settlers as they moved to their own farms, yet the inventory shows two hundred and nine horses in 1942. The extra one hundred and two animals had been purchased by individual settlers from the cash they made as wages working outside the settlement. To the best of my knowledge not very many of the settlers received chickens, sheep or hogs and had to buy them. The same was true for equipment and machinery.

As can be seen from the statistics on the crops, those which were sown were not always the best for the soil and weather conditions. The settlers began to grow more grains to feed livestock.

The large machinery, such as the Caterpillar tractor and land breaking equipment, was owned by the settler who managed the Tate Creek Development Company. It was used less often as the need to break new land decreased, as is shown in the statistics on use of cultivated land.

Close examination of these statistics also shows that many of the items common on farms today were very rare for us. Some of the items were never owned by these pioneer farmers as long as they farmed.

These statistics do not show how much money from the settlement fund was spent on each settler. The following is my calculation of the amount available for the settling of the ninety-five families and twelve single men who were assigned land by 1942.

Resettlement Fund................... $260,000.000
Less: Supervision fee..........$17,050.00
*   Assistance to 59 families*
*   and 25 single men who*
*   left the settlement*
*   before moving to the*
*   land................ $45,000.00 $62,050.00*
Balance............................ $197,950.000

Before settlers were appointed to the board of the company, our representatives were not allowed to see the books of the company, or the monthly reports sent to Winnipeg. In my opinion, the statistics of the company do not give a true picture of what was owned by settlers and by the company in 1942.

In the case of settlers who left the settlement and lost their entitlement to the settlement fund, I have been told that not all received the cost of a one way railway ticket to some city in another part of Canada.

Under settler management, the Tate Creek Development

Company operated until 1955, when it had outlived its usefulness. Procedures for dissolving the company were started and the remaining land holdings, buildings, machinery, and equipment were put up for sale. When all assets had been disposed of, and all liabilities cleared up, only a little over $100 was left for distribution among shareholders.

8

THE FIRST YEAR

The last settlers arrived about the middle of August 1939, and the total population of the settlement, 518 people, became involved in learning to become farmers, learning a new language and suffering from inexperience and primitive conditions. We learned about the harshness of the climate in winter and of the depressed state of the Canadian economy. We became innovative and used the materials available to us to partly overcome the problems and discomforts we were experiencing. A beginning had been made and it was now up to us to make the experiment succeed.

Three activities were of primary importance during the early fall of 1939. It was necessary to finish building houses for the settlers and ensure the houses were weatherproofed before winter came. Only 650 acres of the estimated 15,000 acres of tillable land was cleared and useable for crops; therefore, land clearing and breaking was essential if we were to farm. The livestock which had been purchased to provide fresh milk and meat had to be fed with hay cut in the bush. The department heads organized work parties to do this work.

Men who had gained some skill in using hammer and saw, or were willing to try carpentry were assigned to house building. They helped the native crew, which had been hired by the company to complete unfinished houses and build more. Countless hours were spent on this work. Others were assigned to land clearing or hay making.

My first work assignment was to the haying detail. My work companions were Ernst Pickert, Karl Wagner, and Karl Jellinek. Karl Wagner was the only one among us who had previous experience with that queer looking scythe. We started out about four o'clock in the morning for our first taste of pioneer life in the Canadian bush country. We marched cross-country for about six miles to a place where the bush was full of pea vines and lush grass. On the way we wondered aloud about how to use the queer looking object we carried on our shoulder.

We also wondered how a former auditor, Jellinek; a former political party secretary, myself, and a former porcelain miner, Pickert, would make out as farm laborers. Wagner assured us that despite the queer shape, this type of scythe was very useful in bush, where one was bound to hit the blade on the wood lying around. He told us a European type scythe would never stand up to our task.

When we arrived at our work place, Karl demonstrated how to get a firm grip on the heavy scythe, and the standing position we had to take in order to cut. We tried and tried, but the grass just bent the way we hit it and remained on its stem. So we watched Karl, who was on his second strip before we were able to even make headway for a few feet. If the cows of the settlement had been depending on our production that day, they would have gone hungry.

Besides our struggle with the work, the heat and mosquitoes were almost unbearable. Before we began to work we had rolled up our shirt sleeves, only to pull them down more quickly than we had rolled them up. Bare arms were a welcome invitation to those big hungry mosquitoes. Karl started a controlled fire, on which we threw green branches from the trees to make heavy smoke. When the sun got higher in the late morning, it gave us some relief from the mosquitoes, but the heat became unbearable. In the afternoon, when our scythes became dull we trudged six miles home again.

Early next morning we were on our way again, taking a while to get the aching muscles loosened and the frames of our bodies moving. After we had worked for a couple of hours we noticed that we were starting to do considerably better in our new trade as haymakers.

When we sat down for our lunch break, Karl said that in a few days we would all do as well as he, which, of course, was somewhat of an overstatement. But, we did feel that we were on the way to getting the knack of using this unfamiliar tool, and that perhaps at the end of haying season we might be as expert as Karl. As it turned out, we were sent from place to place, wherever grass for hay could be found. We must have done pretty well. We four haymakers stayed together and we even learned, during that first haying season, how to sharpen our scythes with a file and an emery stone, and they needed sharpening more often than we would have liked in that obstacle-rich bushland. If the cows heard about our exploits, they would have felt a little more confident that we could provide a supplement to the piles of straw for the long cold winter ahead.

Land clearing was tedious, backbreaking work. The men assigned to this job used a pick to dig the soil from around the roots and a long handled axe to cut the roots. When that was done, they put their weight and muscle power against the tree until it started to lean and the weight of the crown brought it down. Trees, such as poplar, did not take much time to bring down with this method. If a tree had a thick heartroot going down into the ground it was more difficult. It was then necessary to dig deep in order to get this root with the axe. Often rocks were lodged close to the troublesome root. One hit with the axe ruined the blade. Much time was lost sitting down with a file trying to put an edge on the axe again.

In time it was learned that the wind could be a great assistant in clearing land. When the prevailing wind from the west was strong, if the roots on the west side of the tree were cut the weight of the crown sometimes was enough to topple the tree.

After the land was cleared a breaking plow was used to turn over the soil. If the clearing crew had done their job well, no stumps interfered with the ploughing; if not, stumps had to be dug out with pick and shovel or pulled out with a team of horses. Rocks and roots thrown up by the plow were picked by hand. The rocks were taken off the new field while the roots were collected and burned. Root and rock picking continued until the field was safe for the seed drill to work without being wrecked by big rocks. We were told that when the land was worked well, a fairly good crop could be expected on a new field.

By the time winter came and breaking of land stopped, the settlers had cleared and broken about 1,000 acres. The following spring 1,650 acres of tillable land in the settlement was prepared and planted by the settlers under the supervision of a Canadian foreman.

We had lived in tents for almost three weeks and walked twelve miles every day to our hay cutting place. One evening, after our daily chore, Alois Mueller came to give us the good news that our frame houses were advanced enough in construction that we could be moved next morning. We were to be moved to the just established Northwest group in the settlement. Mueller, our Hof Marschall (Yard Marshall) a nickname given to him because of his responsibilities for work around the ranch yard, could not have brought better tidings for us that evening. No more cooking in the cook shack because our tents were too small. No more soggy tents and wet floors when it rained. Closer to our hay making places, so no more long walks to work. That evening, we packed our belongings to be ready for an early start.

Being early risers anyway, we were up and ready to move long before the first team and wagon arrived. These moved the women and children. The men stayed, loading the later wagons with household goods as they arrived. I shared a wagon for our belongings with Karl Jellinek. We did not have much besides the tools we were issued and the furniture I had built. There was also a box of clothes and a box with some dishes and kitchen utensils (which we were fortunate enough to have brought from Sweden) as well as some we had been issued when we arrived in the settlement. But Karl, who had lived in Prague, and had had more time and opportunity to bring out his belongings, filled the rest of the wagon with a large wooden box of chinaware and kitchen utensils, some suitcases and boxes filled with clothes, and other items. Ours was the last wagon and was loaded to the hilt when finally, early in the afternoon, it could start to move. We had no other place to perch but on top of the load, like pigeons on a roof.

At that time, there was no road to the new group settlement. The original trail, which had wound through the bush before the clearing and breaking of land, had disappeared. A new trail was being broken across a new field. The ride shook us up as though we were on a stormy sea, on a small ship, at wind strength eleven. But since walking over the rough trail would not have been good either, we stuck it out.

Our empty stomachs were rebelling, since we had not eaten for many hours. The food supplies had been taken by our families early in the morning. In the excitement of getting out of those tents, we had not thought to make sandwiches, for we had no idea that a short trip of six miles would turn out to be so long and hectic.

Everything went along fine as we rumbled across the new breaking. Then it happened, like lightning in a blue sky, the horses shied and started to run. Our driver, not very experienced in handling run-away horses, lost control. From our perch on top we had enough sense to jump before we were thrown off, probably to have been run over.

The runaway team started to circle around the field. The noise of the falling boxes made them even more frantic. After the wagon broke into two pieces, the horses, with the hitch pole between them, ran at a speed that could have put many a race horse to shame.

A box containing my clothes was first to fall off. It broke open and the wind blew my shirts and underwear all over the place, while the team in their circling were trampling on them. When the wagon broke into two parts, the remainder of the load fell off. Karl Jellinek's large wooden box filled with china and kitchen utensils, broke open and spilled dishes all over the place, many of them smashing to pieces.

At first the driver tried to catch the horses, then gave up and sat on the ground out of breath. I was chasing my shirts and underwear! Karl was standing at his broken box wondering aloud what his wife would say. After the driver caught his breath, he went across the field toward another group of settlers, who were picking roots, to ask them for a team and wagon, so we could load up again and move on. In the meantime, Karl and I gathered into a pile anything worthwhile that remained.

It was sunset when the team and wagon finally came, and we could load up and move on. With the long wait and excitement over, we began to realize we still had not eaten. Our stomachs rumbled and we were so hungry that we could have eaten a horse—particularly, one of our runaways.

When we arrived at the new group settlement, we found sandwiches and coffee waiting for us. We unloaded and sorted out our belongings, and learned that the runaway team had been captured only after the hitch pole had stuck between some trees. Living in a tent was behind us, but we could see immediately that we had new problems.

Our eighteen by fourteen frame houses were still without windows, nor had the ceiling or insulated inner walls been put in. The heat of the late summer had widened the cracks by shrinking the fresh lumber, leaving entrances for the mosquitoes and cool night breezes. But just the same, we at least had our own wood cook stove, a board floor under our feet, more room to move around in and, we hoped, a dry roof over our heads.

Construction and finishing of houses continued until all were prepared for winter. Some of the houses in the Northwest group had just had windows put in when the first real cold wave hit us. During the first week of November, when a blizzard covered the settlement with snow, quite a few of the houses were still not winterized. The building crew had yet to insulate them with sawdust mixed with lye — to discourage bugs and rodents — and put up inside walls and ceilings.

During the winter months a community hall was built. Alfred Rei, who had been a carpenter in our homeland and had supervised the building of houses after he arrived, was the architect on this project. The hall was built of logs, which a work crew cut in the forest and another crew hauled to the site. A skilled native carpenter demonstrated to our building crew how logs could be hewn flat on both sides with a broad axe. We all watched as he stretched a colored string along the length of the log, cut a few notches along the log, then with precise strokes of his axe split the length between the notches as smoothly as one would be able to do with a planer. We tried to do the same, but never succeeded in getting such a smooth cut as our native carpenter. It took us much longer to finish a log that was fit to be added to the squares of logs which formed the walls of our hall. The settlers took turns working on the hall. Each settler worked at least one week.

Before spring work started in 1940, the community hall was completed to the stage that it could be used. Settlers meetings, which had been held in the open or in the blacksmith shop, were held there. The hall also made it possible for the settlers to arrange community social gatherings.

Willi Wanka arrived with the last group of settlers and took over the leadership of the settlers committee. While the majority were working at their assigned jobs, Wanka organized some of the preparation for winter. Getting outfitted for winter included buying warm winter clothes for everyone. At the end of August and beginning of September we were invited to the settlement office to have measurements taken for winter garments and after consulting salesmen about the price, Willi Wanka and Valentin Dittrich presented a list of requirements to the settlement supervisor. After several discussions with the supervisor and a reduction in the amount of the order, the clothing was ordered. When the order arrived, neither measurements nor number of items were in accordance with what had been expected. In the end, there were boys' pants left over, and not enough pants for men. Shirts were only in large sizes; nobody was big and fat enough to fit them. Some women received rubber boots but there were not enough for everyone. The rubber boots were finally redistributed, one pair to each family. When an exchange was attempted to correct the order, the answer came back that the delivery had been made in accordance with the order placed and no exchange was possible. After much arguing, the last pieces of missing winter outfits arrived in April 1940, when spring was already in the air. Besides the disappointment about shortages and wrong sizes, we were shocked when we got our first glimpse of the parkas we were to wear. They were a color we all hated, since it sharply reminded us of our enemies, who wore shirts and ties of the same color: BROWN. If there had been at least some variety in the colors it would not have been so bad. But we all, men and women alike, had to run around in parkas of that hated color! We were humiliated and hurt, but could do nothing about it. We hesitated as long as we could before wearing these parkas. But soon, when the temperature dropped to fifty below zero Fahrenheit, we had nothing better to wear. Then we finally put on those hated parkas with sheep skin lining, which gave us at least some protection from the cold, even if they gave no mental comfort.

The shortages and clothing that did not fit forced many of

us to innovate to protect us from the cold. Keeping our feet warm was always a problem that first winter. Some wore moccasins like the Indians, with rags wound around the feet, in addition to socks. I had received a pair of size eleven high rubber boots. My normal size was nine and a half or ten, so I had plenty of room for a number of rags around my feet. The rags made my feet moist from perspiration, which in turn made the rags freeze. That made me hop from one foot to the other in order not to freeze my toes. Later I acquired a pair of moccasins, which were all right if the snow stayed dry. As soon as the snow got wet, the moisture made the rags freeze inside the moccasins and I was in the same predicament again. Later, I wore high felt boots. To protect the felt from getting wet, I pulled rubber galoshes over them, which was all right if the temperatures did not plunge too low. But what is there to wear, at fifty below zero, to simply stay warm?

During our first long cold winter in Canada we began to learn something about our new homeland. Since we were trying to learn to be farmers, our interests were directed toward things agricultural. We learned that an average Canadian farm was two hundred and twenty-three acres, and most of the work on these farms was done with horses and horse-drawn machinery. We also learned of the effects of the depression on farm incomes. A farmer in 1933 would have had to sell thirty-six hides to get enough money to buy a pair of shoes or keep thirty sheep for one year and shear them in order to sell the fleeces for enough money to buy a suit of underwear. From information available to us, we found that industrial workers were no better off. Thousands were unemployed with no hope of getting a job and no unemployment insurance to provide the basics of survival.

The abandoned farms we had seen from the train were the result of the severe drought which had forced thousands of farmers off their land. We began to realize that perhaps we could not all make a living as farmers, even after we learned to farm. Perhaps our skills in trades and professions would be useful after all.

Before the end of our first year in Canada, a school was built in the settlement; some families moved to individual farmsteads, and more land was cleared and broken. We acquired new skills and survived the problems created by our inexperience, and the cold. The experiment of settling non-farmers was not yet a success, but some progress had been made.

9

FRUSTRATION AND HUMILIATION

The establishment and development of our settlement did not always go along smoothly. Our lack of farming experience caused many frustrations as we learned the skills of pioneer farmers. However, our most deeply felt frustration and resentment resulted from the manner in which the settlement supervisors handled the distribution of supplies, the organizing of work and our requests for a variety of items. The problems had begun with the arrival of the first group of settlers. The careless way the kitchen utensils were distributed, the comments about washboards wearing out clothes when these items were requested, and the lack of kerosene for the lamps, were the first indicators of what we were to experience later. The way many settlement matters were handled caused lots of dissatisfaction and arguments among the new settlers. These were understandable but not excusable.

The settlers committee was constantly involved in haggling with the supervisor over items we thought necessary to achieve reasonable standards of hygiene, diet, living accommodation, and enough tools with which to work. Our wives wanted soup ladles to help them in their work; they were told a soup ladle was a luxury and "to use a cup." At one time flour which was not suited for bread making was brought into the company store. A replacement order was made but the new flour contained too much bran and the women still could not bake a decent loaf of bread. They took it back to the store, but the storage facilities were so poor that most of it spoiled and was fed to the livestock. Requests for raisins for cooking and the occasional piece of chocolate for the children were rejected. These were also considered luxury items.

When the first settlers questioned the supervisor about weather conditions and reminded him that the houses had no ceiling or weather proofing on the roof, he shrugged it off by saying that at that time of year it would not rain and the houses would be all right until the roofs could be made rainproof. It did rain. Both food and clothing were spoiled, and the settlers were very uncomfortable in their wet houses.

We also had to haggle with the supervisor to get some fresh vegetables, as the garden vegetables we had grown were placed in poor storage and spoiled. A railway car loaded with vegetables arrived in a heavy snow storm and was unloaded into poor storage where frost did the final damage. The vegetables had cost $600.00 which was charged against the settlers' accounts. I still remember that the sixteen families of the Northwest group received exactly one pail of these vegetables, which we had to divide among us. The remainder, which could not be divided among the other seven or eight settlement groups, was just barely suited to be fed to the livestock. The only exception was cabbage, which was made into sauerkraut and in that way was saved for the settlers.

The potato harvest in 1939 was not distributed among the settlers when it was collected; it was put in storage. The potatoes were distributed after they were frozen. A large portion of these, too, had to be fed to the livestock, while the settlers went without potatoes.

In the late fall of 1939, the settlers' committee made a survey in the settlement and found that the management had handed out more than $1,200.00 worth of tools for which no entries in the books could be found. The bookkeeper did not know what had been handed out, he had not been told about it, and therefore had not recorded it. He had been away much of the time, as he doubled as traveling guide to new arrivals. With new groups arriving at intervals of two or three weeks, he was often away for many days. How could he know what was going on in the office?

At about the same time, the settlers' committee order for winter clothing was presented to the supervisor. He promptly reduced the value of the order from $7,000.000 to $6,000.00. The supervisor personally took the revised order to Edmonton and purchased the clothing. Those hated brown parkas were not selected by the individual settlers or the settlers' committee.

It took weeks to convince the settlement manager that some pocket money for each family was required, since women, in particular, have sanitary needs, and that certain items should be bought by the individual family, according to its needs. An amount of $2.50 per month per family was finally granted.

Smokers went through a hard time during the early weeks of the settlement, when no tobacco could be had. Cigarettes and cigars were such a luxury that, one did not even dare to dream about them in sleep.

The men assigned to look after the distribution of food and milk had difficulty because they did not have the means to do a proper job. Valentin Dittrich, who distributed food supplies, could not give out proper weights when no scale was on hand. An empty can was used until a scale was provided. Josef Tillner could not supply enough milk to the settlers because the number of milk cows was not increased when more people arrived. Often milk cows, purchased to increase the milk production, were no good. Cows which were supposed to be in calf were not.

The supervisor, who directed us in establishing the settlement, also tried to speed up the work. He got the idea that the clearing of the land would go faster if a cutting blade was attached to the caterpillar tractor to cut the trees. That was fine for trees up to four or five inches in diameter because the roots of such trees were not much of a problem for the breaking plow; it had enough power to split the stumps or take them out with the roots on. But it was a different matter with stumps of bigger trees; the plow share bit into the root and all the power of the tractor could not make it budge. The stump had to be left in the ground as a nuisance to operations following the clearing, or else we had to shoulder our picks and axes, and go over the cleared field. We hacked the roots through, then put chains around the stumps and pulled them out with the power of a team of horses.

We cleared one piece of land on section twelve, the Northwest groups' area, by the method the supervisor had thought up. It spoiled the entire process of clearing, and cost us plenty of time and muscle to rectify it later. When the land was broken, the worst mess of roots sticking out or lying around had to be picked by hand and hauled away or burned. Then a heavy disc was used to break up the thick sods left behind. After that, more root picking, before the field was safe for the seed drill.

There was also the problem of breakdowns of the machinery. Many hours were lost on the repairs of the old worn out machinery, which was purchased by the settlement managers. Spare parts for the tractors and machinery were, in too many instances, not on hand and it sometimes took many days to get them. What could not be repaired by welding, just had to wait, and much valuable time was lost in that way. If the management of our settlement had been just a little more proficient our work would have gone along more quickly. But somehow we muddled through with this worn out machinery.

One of the supervisor's biggest blunders affected us seriously in 1940. That year a very promising crop stood in the fields of both the old Tate Creek Ranch and our new fields broken in the previous year. The settlers' committee urged the supervisor to order material for building of more granaries, storage for the upcoming good grain crop. He shrugged off this request saying that in such cases there was never a problem on the Prairies. The grain could simply be threshed on the ground and covered with straw. It would be safe. Several of this type of granary were built by driving poles into the ground, stringing wire mesh around the poles in a circular manner, and lining the inside with black insulation paper. The grain was threshed into these, and covered on top with straw or sheaves of oats.

That fall we had an extended period of heavy rain before freeze up. The rain penetrated deep into the stored grain. When the granaries were opened the following spring, we found a considerable part of the grain was spoiled, even though it had been threshed in nice weather and was dry when stored. This type of granary may have been all right for some region in the Prairies, but it sure was not any good in the Peace River Country.

The settlers, who were struggling to learn how to farm, became very dissatisfied with the way the Canada Colonization

Association representatives were managing our settlement. That we had no agricultural background was not a big handicap because European farming methods would not have fit the conditions in the Peace River country anyway. A little experience with horses, cows, and pigs would have been helpful, but there were few obstacles we did not overcome, given a short period of time. We were mostly people of good educational backgrounds and social standing. Our people had managed large Co-op stores, large trade union locals or had been professionals. We were not like other groups settled by the Canada Colonization Association who had been farmers in Europe. Neither were we laborers permitted into Canada to work on specific jobs, but not welcome as immigrants. We were political refugees who had been accepted as immigrants on the condition that we would become farmers. A fund had been established to cover the cost of our resettlement and we believed it was being wasted. We were not allowed to see our individual accounts and did not know whether items, for which we were charged, were items we had received. We resented being treated in this manner. We even squabbled among ourselves over accounts, sharing of tools and equipment and food supplies. We believed we were being ruled by the divide and conquer method.

Our frustrations were increased when we learned that the hearty welcome the first group of settlers had received in Edmonton was not shared by some German-speaking Canadians. The following editorial appeared in the **Deutsche Zeitung fuer Canada**, on May 24, 1939. This newspaper was established in Winnipeg by a German immigrant who was a Nazi supporter and was funded by the German Consul in Canada. From 1934 to August, 1939, when the government closed it down, the **Deutsche Zeitung fuer Canada** had a whale of a good time spreading Nazi philosophy and defending Hitler's actions. Weekly supplements were published in English which were intended to influence readers to sympathize with Hitler's activities.

We had no means of pointing out the falsehoods or Nazi propaganda contained in this newspaper, and were afraid that the Canadian people might think us traitors not refugees. Our group was very happy to hear that the Canadian press and two members of parliament, Abraham Heaps and J. S. Woodsworth, both from Winnipeg, spoke out against this newspaper. After it was closed down by the government, the editor was arrested and sent to the Kananaskis internment camp.

Sudeten German settlers in Canada were humiliated at the start of World War II, in September 1939. Shortly after Canada got involved in the war, we were notified to report to the RCMP, waiting for us in the office of the management of our settlement. They registered every one of us as enemy aliens. When we heard that, we could not believe that the immigration officials in Ottawa could have had such short memories to have forgotten that we had fled from Nazi persecution; that we had been accepted as political refugees when we entered this country.

Were we, who had fought Nazism and Fascist dictatorships long before the western governments were forced to take up arms against them, enemy aliens? We still could not believe our eyes when we were handed small pieces of paper stating that we were. Many of us, who wanted to join the Canadian forces to take up the fight again, were rejected at the start of the war because of these slips.

We did not sit down quietly and take such humiliation. A meeting was called, and as soon as everybody could be notified we crowded into the blacksmith shop, since no other building was available at the start of our settlement. In that meeting we formulated and all signed a petition, which was sent to the government in Ottawa, to refresh its memory. But the government was busy, thus some time passed before we received attention. I cannot pinpoint the exact date now that so many years have gone by, but my best guess is that it was early in June 1940 when the RCMP, with an apology from the government, went from settler to settler, to collect these, in our eyes, shameful enemy alien slips. After that, the way was open for many of us to join the Canadian armed forces, and to leave the settlement for employment in important war industries. We had many skilled people among us who could now be spared, because there was not enough productive land for all to build up farmsteads.

Many of these so called "enemy aliens" who joined the Canadian armed forces became non-commissioned officers and a few even became commissioned officers. All of them did their share in helping to wrestle down an enemy who threatened to enslave the rest of the free world and hold it under a murderous yoke.

The many skilled tradesmen and industrial workers employed in Edmonton, Vancouver, Toronto, Montreal, Windsor and Hamilton, proved themselves good Canadian citizens, even though they still had to wait for their citizenship papers.

The Sudeten Settlers and other Canadians have since learned that Prime Minister Mackenzie King had been favorably impressed by Hitler when they met in 1937. In recently published parts of Mr. King's diary he stated: "He (Hitler) is particularly strong on beauty, loves flowers, and will spend more of the money of the state on gardens and flowers than most other things." Did Mr. King not hear the rumbling sounds of German armament plants running in high gear? Or of Adolf Hitler's economic Czar and Luftwaffe Minister, Herman Goering, who declared over and over again in his speeches to the German people:"Cannons are more important than butter."

The fascination of the Prime Minister of Canada for the German dictator went so far that King's diary tells of him having said to Hitler that he and his Ministers had been prejudiced against Hitler and his policies which they had believed were narrow views, and nationalist and imperialistic in purpose. Mackenzie King further stated that: "We all came to feel quite differently, and believed policies towards European countries would be wisely administered in his (Hitler's) hand." After returning to Canada Mr. King wrote in his diary that: "I have come away from Germany tremendously relieved. I believe that there will be no war."

It is difficult to understand how Mr. King was so grossly naive about the reality of the political situation in Germany during the thirties. His opinions then were symptomatic of the thinking of other leaders of western nations, just as his government's declaration of German immigrants as enemy aliens was symptomatic of thinking in 1939. Those who have experienced these realities can only hope that by exposing them it will not happen again.

Our humiliation ended with removal of our enemy alien cards. Our frustration with the poor management of our settlement was not entirely over when, in the spring of 1942, the first supervisor was replaced by H. J. Siemens. Siemans was a more reasonable man but he arrived too late to correct all the blunders made by his predecessor.

10

OUR OWN FARMS

Following the settlement meeting, when we learned some of us would be moved to our own land, each group settlement was assigned land surrounding their small settlement. The families in the Northwest group, where I lived, held a meeting to choose our land and the families with whom we wanted to share work and equipment. As a rule, we had talked about these choices beforehand, and the meeting was just a formality.

The decision to move families to their own land had been made in mid-winter, when the land was under a deep cover of snow. About the beginning of February, we began wading through the snow to get a glimpse of our quarter sections in order to select the spot for a house and a barn.

My land was the northeast quarter of Section 13, Township 23. I shared that section with Karl Jellinek, Frank Schoeder, and Ernst Pickert. There was no point on this section where we could have moved our houses together, still have them on our own land, and have easy access to water. There was a creek on the extreme west side and another flowed through the southwest side. My neighbor on the west side could get his water from the creek cutting across a corner of his property, and Frank Schoeder and Ernst Pickert could get water from the creek running through Schoeder's land. I had only the hope of getting mine from a large muskeg, until a dugout could be scooped to collect the spring runoff and the water from rains.

When a site had been selected and warmer weather returned, the houses could be moved. The houses were built so they could be transported by slipping long logs beneath them. When a house was ready to be moved, five or six men were called together to lift it up. This was done with a long heavy spruce pole, flattened on the thick end so it would not roll when the men used their weight and muscle strength to lift one corner. Then other men put props under it, to hold it. By repeating this procedure several times on all four corners, the house was high enough to slip long spruce logs under it. That done, two thick planks were nailed across both ends of these logs to prevent them from moving together when the house was let down onto them. After heavy logging chains were attached at the front, the houses were moved by a heavy diesel caterpillar, or by two other heavy tractors. If a porch or some lean-to was attached, these had to be moved separately or taken apart before the house was moved. Those built with poles could be put together again, when the house was on its new location. All of the belongings a family had acquired since they had come to Canada were moved inside the house. Sometimes the women even prepared food for the moving crew in the house-on-the move.

Karl Jellinek and I hacked out a trail through the bush wide enough for our fourteen foot wide houses to be pulled through. We cleared the trail together to a point where my neighbor turned west. I turned east and carried on clearing a trail to the spot where I intended to have the house moved, and where I had already built a shelter out of spruce poles for my livestock. The site was on the highest of two hills. I had chosen the site for the view of the valley.

Toward the end of April 1940, the spring break up started, and with it the moving of our houses. Everything went fine until we had to cross one of the spring runoff water courses. The water had softened the ground and the caterpillar tractor pulling the house got stuck. It took more chains and a lot of maneuvering before the outfit started to move again. By keeping to ground heavily covered with willows, giving the caterpillar some hold, it could work slowly forward up the gentle slope of the hill.

We ran into another of these water runoffs at the foot of the high portion of the hill. All the willows around did not help, and the caterpillar with the house behind it failed to advance another foot. It was stuck so deep in the churned up ground that the house had to be unhitched, since the logs on which the house sat were buried in deep ruts. The house was touching the ground and would have torn apart if moved any further. I was told that the house must remain on that spot until the ground dried up enough so that moving could be resumed in about a week.

It was late evening by then, and everybody involved in the adventure was hungry and tired. I was not only tired, but boiling mad the house had not been moved a few days earlier, while the ground was still frozen. I thought it was inexcuseable that the supervisors had not given us greenhorns some sensible advice before we made such blunders, but they left matters up to us to find out the hard way. I was certain that the house was sitting on my assigned land, and told the mover that the house was not going to be moved up the hill, but was to stay right on the spot where we got stuck. As it turned out later, that was the best decision I had ever made in anger and frustration. When the snow disappeared the house was closer to my water supply in the muskeg. I realized later that it was probably the best location on my land to build a farmstead.

All I could do for the rest of that evening was to take my axe and clear the willows from around the stuck house, in order to get the door open. All next day I kept busy clearing more bush from around the house, which could have made one seasick at the sight of it, the way it was leaning. The movers came back and gave me a hand in propping it up. We finally got the house set level, with the help of many props.

That first winter it was very awkward walking up the steep hillside to the livestock shelter to feed and milk the cows. I must say now that it served me right. I should have used my head and selected a location for my house and barn for practical living, not for the grand view from the hill. Who had time, in those years, for viewing the scenery when 365 days of the year were filled from early morning until late in the evening with hard work?

In the case of Frank Suttner, it took almost two weeks to get the house moved because heavy rains had softened the ground on the long trail through the bush to a lake, where Frank's land was located. Ditches, deepened by swift running water had to be spanned by bridges, which were time-consuming to build. To do this heavy logs were dragged by horses across the ditches, then poles were cut and nailed to the beams, so it would be strong enough to carry the load of tractor and house. The Suttner family had to keep house in the middle of the trail until conditions improved enough to continue the moving of their house. Many other inconveniences and mishaps occurred on these moves, but to my recollection Frank Suttner's case was the worst.

Seventy-four other settlers and I eventually got to our land with our houses. We could then start farming with our shared equipment and horses, one bred sow and three cows.

With the move to our own farms we thought we would become self-sustaining in a very short time. From spring to fall in 1940, we were busy building barns from logs cut in the bush; building lean-tos for our frame shacks, to give us a little more room; clearing more land; picking roots and rocks, and cutting hay for the livestock.

After getting my house propped up, I began to clear the bush from the land so that it could be broken by company owned equipment. When I started clearing my second piece of land I wondered how many trees I would have to take off this particular piece. It was located on a hillside with only light growth, which I figured would not be difficult to clear. The poplars were small and no digging of roots would be necessary. Looking down the hill side, I saw empty spaces between groups of trees beyond the lightly wooded area. I thought I could gain more land by including this piece in my clearing plan. I measured the area with a pole I had cut into a rod. The enlarged piece would give me about fifteen acres instead of eight or nine. Elated by this discovery I set to work. As I had always had a flair for and interest in statistics I kept a daily record of how many trees I cut. After many days of hard work, I added up the list I had kept. I found to my surprise that I had cleared more than 800 trees to achieve my goal of fifteen acres.

I cleared twenty-five acres in the summer of 1940, and another fifteen in 1941/42. We had been promised that twenty acres of our land would be broken as soon as it was cleared. I got no land broken until late in 1941. By that time I was in debt for close to $300.00 and had to take credit from the Canada Colonization Association. I had not received the pregnant sow promised each settler, which would have provided some income for me. In the winter of 1941/42 I worked in the lumber camp, operated by the company, so I could pay back some of this debt.

Others had similar experiences, when their land remained unbroken or they did not receive the promised livestock. They often took laboring jobs away from their farms to provide a livelihood for their families. Some men worked for farmers who came to the settlement to get help in 1940 and 1941, when farm labor was scarce because of the war. They earned money stooking and threshing other farmers' grain crops. Work on the Alaska highway began in 1942, and many of the settlers worked on that project.

Water became a very serious problem for the Northwest group during the hot dry summer of 1939. The two small creeks running through the section I shared were, by July, only trickles. In August, there were only some pools of water left. These became stale and awful-smelling under the hot sun. The water we got from these pools was full of bugs and had to be boiled before it could be used. We then squeezed lemon juice into it to make it drinkable. To keep the water cool, I recall digging a hole on the north side of our shack and placing a covered pot or jar in it.

We learned that in other groups in the settlement drilling for water was going on; in some cases water was found. Even though we knew that sometimes the water found tasted of minerals, we went to the settlement office to find out if our group would get a well drilled.

Shortly after that one of the supervisory personnel came out, accompanied by another man. This man started to witch for water with the willow branch he held in his hand. The forked willow branch was held in front of the person. The claim was that the prongs of the branch would bend down when there was water below the ground. The witcher claimed he could feel a strong downward pull on his hands. Not far from the dried up creek, about the center of our line of shacks, the man stopped, put a stake into the ground and declared, "Here is water." About a week later a well driller arrived with his equipment. The equipment looked to me like something on loan from a museum in another world. I recall helping the driller to lift the handles of the drilling rod and letting it drop to punch a hole in the earth and bring out the soil. When some moist soil came up after many hours of this hard exercise, the driller exclaimed: "I think we are hitting a big spring."

The drilling operation went on and every day the driller enthusiastically said that today we would find water. After weeks of hard work the operation was a failure. I don't think that we ever would have found water in that spot unless we tapped some lake on the other side of the globe. Our source of water remained the stale pools in the creek, the lake near the Tupper station, or dugouts along the edge of the muskeg. In winter, drinking water was available by melting blocks of ice from the lake. Snow was often melted for washing clothes and watering livestock.

Other shortages were somewhat more easily overcome. Those who had livestock and were short of meat sometimes butchered an animal. Learning to do this for the first time resulted in some humorous incidents.

One day a settler had run out of meat. He had inherited a boar from the settlement management which was not living up to his duties. The settler decided that the big, fat, lazy animal could be transformed into pork sausages, lard, head cheese, pork chops, and lots of smoked hams.

He sharpened his knives and prepared plenty of scalding water in a steel barrel, which was needed to get off the bristles. Then he carefully sneaked up from behind his victim, who had been let out of his pen and was dozing in a shady spot near the building, and delivered a hard blow with the blade of an axe to the forehead of the animal. Confident that he had killed the boar with one stroke, the farmer ran to pick up one of his sharpened knives to stick and bleed the dead animal. As the would-be butcher stuck his knife in where a pig is supposed to be cut open for bleeding, the enraged boar jumped up and started to chase the frightened farmer all over the place.

The chase ended with the farmer on top of his rickety outhouse to escaped the enraged boar. The animal still had the butcher knife sticking in his neck and was trying to reach the man. The terrified man shouted to a neighbor for help. When the neighbor finally heard the distressed man, he came running with his rifle, ended the misery of the poor suffering boar and rescued the man from his peculiar refuge. Had the boar known that a good push with his snout would have overturned the flimsy outhouse and its load, who knows what the end of that first butchering adventure would have been. The settler and his family enjoyed the many hams and sausages for several weeks after this incident.

We did learn about farming. Sometimes the hard way. Those who had some European farming experience knew how to milk a cow, or harness and drive a team of horses, which gave them a slight advantage. When it came to Canadian farm machinery we were all equally ignorant. Those who succeeded were those who realized, at an early stage, that Canadian farming was very different from European farming. In many cases, those with no farming experience became successful farmers. We did not become prosperous immediately but we did become self-sufficient in just a few years.

11

HAZARDS

The weather was dry and hot during the summer of 1940. Burning of brush had to be stopped for if the tinder dry top soil caught fire, it was not easy to extinguish. West and north of our settlement, we had for many weeks watched black smoke billowing over the horizon. A bush fire was advancing from the direction of Pouce Coupe. We knew that this fire was a serious threat and had to be stopped. But this settlement stayed lucky until the early fall.

A fire started on Gust Schneider's land. It burned harmlessly for a while before it was discovered, because of the smoke coming into the settlement from distant fires. Then it spread over four sections, endangering the farmsteads of twelve settlers and advancing close to some. It became a hell of a big and dangerous fire!

We, in the northwest area, did not realize how big and dangerous it was because the heavy bush and hilly landscape blocked our view. We were busy with our own work when the settlement supervisors came rushing out with truck and their cars. They told us about the fire. We picked up our picks, shovels and axes and went off to fight the fire.

When we reached the fire we found that sometimes a tree branch did more good snuffing out the flames in the burning grass than our tools. We worked frantically to stop the flames which endangered a house or barn. We had to break into one house and take the belongings to safety in the community hall when we thought we were going to be unable to overcome the fast advancing flames.

The wind calmed down during the evening and we were able to start counter fires. Our small fires burned slowly toward the on-coming big one. It was after midnight when the opposing fires met and burned themselves out. We were fortunate that none of the settlers lost their homes or barns. As we walked home exhausted, we felt richer from our frightening experience.

We were not always so lucky when the weather conditions threatened our settlement; nor did we feel richer from those experiences.

The fields in the settlement in the early summer of 1941 looked like a farmer's dream with a bumper crop in the making. Then all of a sudden nature played one of its pranks on us by dumping several feet of wet snow on the landscape in the middle of August. It buried under its heavy weight everything that had been standing up with such promise. This snowfall, combined with freezing temperatures the next few nights, made the disaster appear complete.

When this unseasonal storm was over and the snow had melted away, the uncut grain, some of which was in the ripening stage, lay twisted in all directions, and flat on the ground. Some barley had already been cut and the sheaves were lying on the fields waiting to be stooked. But there was hope that the snow was protection against frost, and that the grain could be harvested somehow — even though at that time nobody knew how.

Our hopes were dampened by rainstorm after rainstorm before the fields had a chance to dry after the heavy snow storm. It rained on and off for six weeks. Before the fields could dry out enough to carry horse drawn harvesting machines, night frosts came, sealing the heavy heads of the grain stalks in the wet ground.

After it became clear to the management of the settlement that harvesting with binders was impossible, the large communally owned fields were divided into parcels. It was to be harvested by those settlers who had not had land broken the year before, when they moved to their assigned quarter sections.

We used any tools available to do the job. Some settlers who were able to get a hayrake, used it to tear the grain loose from the frozen ground to let it dry in windrows for threshing. Others, who did not have a hayrake, or thought that this method would not work on their parcel, sharpened their scythes and went to work. I was one of these, and I had by then, become fairly handy with one of those funny looking Canadian scythes.

I was assigned ten acres to harvest — five acres of oats and five of barley. A neighbor and I worked together on our parcels. We had to cut the oats, gather it up, and tie it into sheaves. Then we set the sheaves into a stook to dry. The barley, which had been cut but not stooked before the rain and snow set in, lay in soggy sheaves on the ground. We had to pick up the sheaves and set them into stooks. Each time we picked up a sheaf, we got soaking wet. We lost quite a number of bushels of barley by having to pry loose the sheaves, which were frozen to the ground.

When we finally got our harvest threshed after all the hard work, it yielded me a little over 200 bushels of oats and a smaller amount of barley. I was very angry about that. If those who were entitled to the harvest had been assigned the work earlier much more of the grain could have been saved.

I was among the few lucky ones who had their threshing done on Christmas eve 1941. Another snow storm came up before we finished unloading the last sheaves into the grain separator. The damp sheaves caused the machine to clog up several times before they went through. I had the final load of grain on my wagon and was on my way home when it turned cold and the snow came down more thickly than before. No more threshing was done that year.

This disasterous harvest caused a shortage of feed for the livestock. To ease this shortage, the management bought stacks of hay from farmers near Limburn, Alberta. Settlers were sent to pick it up with teams of horses and hayracks on sleighs. The weather was very cold. Rain, followed by frost, had made the haystacks a solid mass which had to be cut with axes. Even hay knives failed to penetrate the stack.

After a tedious day of hacking out the hay, loading it, and eating frozen lunches, the sleigh train started back to the settlement. They arrived at the settlement in the early hours of the next day. When the hay was fed to the cows, they just sniffed at it and walked away. The horses, who as a rule will eat roughage a cow does not touch, only picked at the mass put before them. The hay was rough grass that had grown in sloughs and even hungry livestock would not eat it. The long hayride in sub-zero weather turned out to be a big flop, and many more long trips had to be taken to areas where strawstacks were made available to us by friendly farmers.

I learned that a farmer west of Dawson Creek had some feed grain for sale. He also had some strawstacks he did not need himself and was willing to give away. I needed the straw because the rail fences I had built around my haystacks had been no deterrent to herds of deer and moose and the thousands of rabbits. These animals had eaten or trampled their droppings into the wild hay that I had cut and stacked before the bad weather set in. Thus there was not much left to feed my livestock by early spring. The grain I had left for my few pigs was only enough for two or three weeks of feeding. Early one cold morning in 1942, I harnessed the team of horses I had that week for my work and drove the forty-odd kilometers to get some feed for my livestock.

My good friend and neighbor Ernst Pickert went along with me. The wheels of the hayrack rattled over the rough frozen road as we passed through Pouce Coupe and Dawson Creek. It was cold enough that our lunches froze. As we passed the Chinese restaurant in Pouce Coupe we thought about stopping for a warm meal; neither of us had enough money. I knew forty bushels of feed wheat was going to cost forty cents per bushel and that was all I had. Instead we put some of our lunch in our inner pockets, close to our bodies to thaw.

The weather warmed up before we arrived at the farm, and we were glad to take off our parkas. We shovelled the grain into bags and loaded it onto the hayrack. We then filled the remaining space with straw. It was afternoon when we started back. The horses huffed and puffed under the heavy load on the now muddy road. We hoped it would freeze again so that we would be able to tackle the high hill between Pouce Coupe and our settlement.

When we reached the hill in the evening, water was still running down it. The wheels of the wagon sank deeper into the mud until we were hopelessly stuck. We rested the horses, and with both of us pushing with all our might, still could not move the wagon a single foot ahead. There was only one thing left for us to do: unhitch the team and tie them to a tree, while we carried half our sacks a half-mile down the hill to a nearby farm, for a few days keep.

That done, we loaded the straw back on the wagon again. After leading the horses down the hill for a drink from the creek, we hitched up and tried again. The horses were more rested then, and with some shouting and encouragement, they succeeded in pulling the wagon out of the mud. Now we could carry on home, since it was late evening, and the ground had started to freeze again.

Our experiences with these hazards vividly showed us the true character of the climate. We now knew that the abandoned farms we had seen from the train were only one reality in farming. The realities of our new vocation in the bushland became very clear to us with each new experience.

12

A COMMUNITY DEVELOPS

The buildings of the Tate Creek Ranch were located four miles northwest of the Tupper railway station. The ranch buildings became the center of the settlement where the Canada Colonization Association store, butcher shop, school, community hall, and a Roman Catholic church were all located.

Our essential supplies of grocery goods, at the start of the settlement, were handled in the company store. Valentin Dittrich, who had been appointed by the settlement management to distribute goods, had very little say as far as ordering was concerned. Before the transfer of authority to the settlers themselves it had been decided by the Settler's Committee to form a Co-op. The management of the settlement was not very enthusiastic about the plan in the beginning, but finally were persuaded to allow the plan to be carried out. They assisted by turning over their inventory of $4,270.00 as a credit to the new Co-op. This, with the shares of the members, financed the new operation.

Valentin Dittrich became the first manager of the Tate Creek Co-op store. Its success was apparent when, after the first year of operation, the credit of $4,270.00 was paid back to the settlement company. The annual report of the Co-op to the members for the year 1943 showed a turnover in business of $37,263.00, which at that time could be considered very good. The turnover increased from year to year as the financial situation of the members improved.

Besides the company store, a settler, Josef Weinhart, was allowed to open a butcher shop in the winter of 1939/40, to provide fresh meat, sausages, and other meat products. That was done only after complaints and dissatisfaction among the settlers had reached proportions that the management could no longer ignore.

The butcher shop helped considerably, but it was not the solution to our problems in the supply of essentials. Business for Weinhart's butcher shop declined as individuals started to do their own butchering, with the increase of their livestock. The shop closed after two years, and the Co-op brought in smoked meats and sausage to improve the meat supply.

In the beginning the Co-op management made an arrangement with a livestock shipper in Hythe, Alberta, to handle settlers shipments. Later livestock shipping was handled by the Co-op itself. Every second Friday settlers brought their hogs and other livestock to a corral at the railway station, where it was weighed by Mr. Dittrich, a receipt given to the seller, and then shipped to Edmonton. About one week later, settlers could pick up their cheques from the packing companies at the Co-op store. The livestock shipping operation of the Co-op was reasonably successful, achieving a turnover of more than $115,000 in its first three years.

The Co-op store also served as our post office, as it was not very convenient for the settlers to pick up mail at the Tupper post office twice a week. Eventually that caused too much work for the storekeeper, as the volume of mail increased and another solution had to be found.

I am sure neither Karl Jellenick or I dreamed, in 1940, that the trail we hacked through the bush before moving our houses would become our road. This and other primitive roads were a constant problem to settlers. I recall being stuck in the many low spots on these trails hundreds of times. The wooden culverts and bridges built by the settlers often could not carry all the loads hauled across them. If a Caterpillar tractor went over them it sometimes took some logs with it. Every year, particularly in the spring, there were washouts which had to be fixed, new culverts to be built, an old one made larger or a rotten one to be replaced.

As soon as we moved to our land, we became responsible for payment of land taxes. Our cash income was barely enough to get by on, and though the taxes were not very high, often we could not afford to pay them. The government of British Columbia had a provision which allowed small farmers to pay their taxes in kind, which meant working them off on roadwork.

In our settlement there was plenty of road work for all, when new dirt roads were plowed and graded. Not all roads were immediately improved. The road from the old highway, which passed through the community center to the northwest district was improved so that a school bus could use it. It was not until after the war that this road, west and north of my farmstead, was upgraded and gravelled making it almost useable all year round.

Until then, often a trip of a few miles could sometimes take a full day. This happened to me while I was hauling a load of barley home in 1941. I tried to avoid the worst mudhole, where I knew I would get stuck for sure, and instead drove through a slough, where willows would give me some support. I was just a few feet from the farthest edge of the slough when my team gave up. The wagon sank deeper and deeper into the soft ground. I had to walk to the nearest farm for help, but no one was home. Then I had to walk back again, and then in the opposite direction until I was luckier and found help. With two teams, and several trials, we succeeded in getting the load of grain out of the mudhole and moving again. I had expected to be home by noon that day, but it was late in the evening when I finally arrived.

Our settlement was twenty miles from the nearest doctor or dentist. During the early stages of the settlement, when we had no adequate means of transportation, this was often a problem. Dr. Arnold Glass, who had been a doctor in Prague, could not practice medicine in Canada because he did not then have a license. However, he often looked after emergency cases. He had brought his instruments with him and established an office in the lean-to attached to his house, located in the community center. As I recall, the most outstanding pieces of furniture were a large chair and some shelves the doctor had built with some pieces of two by four's.

I became one of Dr. Glass' emergency cases when a toothache cost me the loss of two nights sleep and I could no longer stand the pain. In spite of my eagerness to get rid of the pain from that troublesome molar, the sight of the chair brought goose pimples to my skin. My feelings of fright were not lessened when the doctor told me that he had instruments for pulling my teeth, but that he had nothing for freezing because he could not get drugs without a license to practice medicine. I remember stammering "I can't stand the horrible pain any longer, you must do something." The doctor answered that it was entirely up to me what I preferred—the toothache or the pain of pulling the tooth. Weighing the future nights of pain against the short excruciating pain of having the tooth pulled without freezing, I decided on the latter and sat down on my doctor friend's torture chair. I cannot recall at what point the doctor picked up his instruments and said, "open your mouth —open it wide", but before I had a chance to let out a scream, he was handing me a bowl to catch the blood running out of my mouth. The doctor doused a wad of cotton with some disinfectant and stuffed it in my wound.

He told me to keep my mouth shut on the way home so I would not get a cold in my wound. As I walked the six miles home, I recall hoping for a better night than the ones I had behind me.

Because Dr. Glass was not allowed to practice medicine immediately, many settlers suffered more than necessary from the lack of proper medical facilities. Dr. Glass did the best he could for us under the circumstances.

The development of individual farms did not occur in an even pattern with the result that differentiation within the settlement occurred. There were a great many factors involved which influenced the future of individual settlers. Among these factors were the location of his land, the quality and quantity of the livestock and equipment he received, the structure of his family, the amount of cleared or cultivated land on the quarter section he had selected when the land contracts were signed. In dealing with some of these factors, I shall start with the structure of the individual families, as I believe it to be very important.

If the children of a family were small and still needed lots of attention from their mothers, that had a rather hampering effect on the development of the family farm. Time and energy were diverted from the chores on the farmstead to raise children. If the children were in their teens when they arrived with their parents, they were a great asset. They not only could help with building up the farmstead but could also work on an outside job to help their family financially.

Another factor which influenced differentiation was the location of the land. If the land was located on high ground, the danger of early frost was less acute than it was in low-lying fields. Fields close to muskeg or sloughs were often damaged by frost in August.

It also made a difference if one was lucky enough to get better machines or better livestock than his neighbor. Or if his brood sow farrowed a large litter of piglets at the early stage of settlement, while his neighbor had a sow which was either not pregnant as had been claimed, or produced only a small litter, or squashed them at farrowing.

If one was so lucky as to have open wild hay land on his quarter section, that was also an advantage. Livestock could be fed at less cost than that of a neighbor who had to clear bushland and pay the cost of breaking before he could grow a crop of clover or brome grass.

Another important factor was the amount of cultivated acreage a settler had on his quarter section when the land contracts were signed. Sometimes the price of one man's land could be double the price of his neighbor's, or more. For example, a quarter section of land with twenty acres of land broken cost, say, $320.00 while another quarter section with perhaps forty-five or fifty acres broken cost, say, $800.00. Each settler received a credit of $250.00 from the settlement fund toward the cost of land. The first settlers would be indebted to the company for only seventy dollars, while the second settler's debt would be $550.00. Even though the first settler had a smaller debt, he still had to pay the costs of clearing and breaking thirty acres before the two were on equal terms. The cost of clearing and breaking were charged to settlers at the rate of eight and fifteen dollars per hour, respectively, in 1946. These costs had to be taken into account along with yearly land payments before a family could gain a decent living.

The quality of the soil was not the same in every corner of the settlement and made a difference in the number of bushels of grain which were produced in any year. The skill and knowledge the individual settlers acquired in making the right choice of the varieties of crops he grew on his land, also made a difference. We all had to learn farming more or less by trial and error.

Our community hall, built during the first winter of our settlement, was gradually improved as time and money permitted. For smaller meetings an extra room was built. There was also a room set aside for our first library, which found many eager users during the winters.

Politics which had always played a very important part in our lives and was the reason we had become refugees, contributed to the differentiation within the settlement. A small action group believed, a few years after our arrival in Canada, that the settlement would derive advantages and favors from the ruling Liberal and Conservative coalition government in British Columbia if we, new voters, instead of favoring the party closest to our own views, voted Liberal. The writer vehemently rejected such political opportunism and is still of the opinion that in a democracy one should not fall into such manoeuvers out of fears or for political convenience, but should stand on principles, unless one honestly arrives at other political views. One should never try to have it both ways.

We had all fled our homeland because of our steadfast belief in freedom and democracy. We rejected all forms of dictatorship and I would fight in my new homeland too against any form of discrimination. Neither would I ever exchange, for group or personal benefit, my belief in freedom and my choice of political party, regardless of which party holds power. The base for true democracy is the right of free choice. If this right is violated by corrupting political favoritism, it too must be fought as foreign to true democracy. That some of the Sudeten settlers, under the strain of living in hard new conditions, abandoned these principles, is regrettable. But that has to be taken as just one more of those things which, in the history of political emigrations, had often happened. Ours will not have been the last of such regrettable occurrences. Life in political asylum, I believe, requires more moral fiber than life under normal conditions.

Our new settlement and developing community did not escape personal tragedy. Willi Brenner, a single man, who had worked in the uranium mines in St. Joachimstal, in the Sudetenland, brought lung cancer to Canada with him. This was an occupational disease of many of the miners in St. Joachimstal. The average life span of these uranium miners was only thirty-five years. Before Dr. Glass could obtain the necessary medicine, Willi Brenner in 1940, unable to endure his suffering any longer, ended his own life.

Had Willi Brenner been able to stay in his homeland, he would have received early treatment for his disease and would not have had to endure such suffering. Not only that, early treatment would have prolonged his life. The young uranium miner from St. Joachimstal can be numbered among those who had to die because a regime in his homeland opposed the principles of freedom and decency.

Tragic as the death of Willi Brenner was, another case in the same year was not less so. Another settler who could not stand the pressures of the new environment, and the strange and new living conditions we all faced, took his own life.

Next was the death of a small baby in a house fire. The mother had gone to a neighbor's when it happened. An extra strong draft caused the soot in the pipes of the sheet metal heater to catch fire, igniting the dry lumber of the ceiling. When the fire was noticed, the mother, with the neighbor, ran to the house to try to save the baby but it was too late. The fire took only minutes to engulf the frame shack, which had no proper chimney, only the stove pipe leading through the ceiling protected by a piece of sheet metal.

The community continued to develop in all ways, as the settlers overcame the primitive conditions and lack of goods and services. Differentiation in both the economic and political matters continued, but in spite of this we became a community with pride in our achievements and sorrow for our losses.

13

EDUCATION AND LANGUAGE

When we arrived at Tupper station in 1939, few of us had any knowledge of English. Some of the adults and children, who had spent time in England, had picked up a few words. Those of us who had temporarily lived in other European countries had none. Our children learned the new language in school, while some adults struggled to learn it by other means. We were often frustrated by the language problem, but sometimes our experiences were humorous.

We were afraid at first that a school would not get built during the frantic building activity going on in the summer of 1939. One was built, and in the late fall the children of the settlement started their education. Some of the children went to schools already in operation at Tupper and the hamlet of Gundy. Teaching these children was not an easy task. But young children learn pretty fast and with the help of their teachers were soon able to take part in competitions with children of other communities. They brought to the settlement many certificates and prizes won in these competitions. The following excerpt from an article by Gordon McCallum of the **Edmonton Journal**, written in August 1939, describes one of the children's first teachers, whom I recall.

"Because she was a refugee herself, Miss E. C. Meade who is to be one of three school teachers for the children of the Sudeten refugee settlers near Tupper, B.C., finds it easy to sympathize with these people who have left a nightmare behind but who are finding happiness in Canada. Miss Meade, who is proud because none of her students has broken a school window for nine years, was in Tokyo when an earthquake rocked the city in 1923. And she promptly became a refugee from disaster, arrived in Victoria without a nickel and got a job on that city's teaching staff.

"From there she went to Rose Prairie in the B.C. section of the Peace River Block, then to the Sudeten settlement. She asked for the teaching job, and promptly got it from school Inspector A. B. Towel of Pouce Coupe, who is in charge of all B. C. Schools in the Peace River block.

"Miss Meade, born in England, was in Japan teaching American, English and Canadian children their A.B.C.'s when the earthquake came. She had been there just 10 months.

"When she was being shipped home as a refugee, she decided she liked Victoria, got the teaching job, stayed eight years.

"She took time out during those eight years to organize a school at Shelley, B.C. near Prince George. That was before she learned to like the cold. She slept in an old bunk house which once was occupied by a Chinese.

"And it was so cold that I took my puppy and hot water bottle to bed with me" she said.

"Now she keeps a window open all year round, can't stand it if she has more than one blanket. She rides a horse named Chinook who got his name because he's a dirty gray, and chinooks always turn the nice white snow to a dirty gray.

"She wears spurs. She jingles like a Royal Canadian Mounted Policeman when she walks. She has been at the Rose Prairie school, north of the Sudeten settlement, for six years. Now she's going to this new job and is sure that "it's going to be fascinating work. My, I will really enjoy it."

"She bubbles over with enthusiasm, spurs her horse to action when she finds cows wandering in an oatfield.

"I can understand German a little,' she said. 'Just enough as a matter of fact, to be of great assistance. If I knew more German it would not be so good because it would be too easy to turn to that language. Instead, I know just enough to be able to understand the difficulties of these people so I can help them in their education work.

"Three teachers will be named to teach the 90 children of the Sudeten families. The other two have not been named yet.

"All three will be working nearly every night teaching

adults their reading and writing, but not much arithmetic. It's English the adults want.

"Miss Meade's school is being built now and will be ready on Sept. 5—unpainted, probably, but still a school with first-class desks and other equipment. Meanwhile, she's living with the Sudetens, learning their ways, becoming friends with the adults, letting the children ride her horse. Pupils will not be afraid of their teacher when the term opens.

"I am getting to know them real well," she said. "I always have had the opinion that it is well to know the children both in and out of the classroom." Miss Meade will do the day and evening work for a whole year for $930.00.

"She will board herself, too, leaving school at 4:00 p.m. and hurrying home to prepare her evening meal. Early every evening she will be back at school to teach the adults.

"One of her special students will be Dr. Arnold Glass. She will teach him English so that some day he can quit being a farmer and become a doctor again, as he was back in pre-Hitler Prague.

"In other words, this country school teacher, who loves her work, to a large degree holds the professional future of a skilled medical man in her capable hands.

"Mr. Towell, whose official title is Director of Education for the B.C. section of the Peace River district is enthusiastic, too, at the opportunity of being of service to these little ones from far lands. He is proud of his district, proud of Miss Meade, proud of the medical services which are given to the 1400 children in the block.

"Miss Meade's school," he said, "was one of the best schools in the block last year. And I am sure that she will be of valuable assistance in her new work here."

The honors obtained in competition with children from other schools must be credited to Miss Meade and her assistants. The later success of the first settlers' children, must also be credited to them.

Arnold Glass became a doctor again, and practised for several years in Hythe, Alberta.

The settlement of a certain language group of immigrants in a close community has some advantages. In our case, speaking our own language made us feel more secure while learning our new vocation, and made it easier. On the other hand, it was a disadvantage in learning the language of the country. I believe, that in our case, more effort could have been made by the British Columbia government, the Immigration Department in Ottawa, and the settlement administration to help us learn English. Unlike other immigrants, who had come from cities and went to cities, we were forced to live in a designated area without proper facilities to learn the language. After an eight hour workday, others could attend evening classes and improve their chances for better jobs. Even if they had to start at the bottom in a job in which language did not matter so much and provided only a meager livelihood, it was a starting point to a better life.

Only a small number of the settlers could attend the evening classes at the school. The majority of settlers lived many miles distant from the school. At the start of the settlement there were no roads which would have deserved that name. The only means of transportation was the one horse and half a wagon or sleigh the settlers received when they moved to their assigned land. After working long days on the land, who could have been expected to walk six to ten miles to an evening class and back home again. Most of the adult settlers tried to learn English by other methods.

As soon as we could afford subscriptions to English language farm newspapers, we subscribed in the hope that by trying to read the language we would get a better feeling for it when we heard it spoken by the supervisors. When the temperature fell too low, forbidding outdoor work, and our daily chores were done, we sat down near our sheet metal heaters and tried to read our newspapers.

I found that this method of learning English did not do too much good when, in the late spring of 1942, I joined the Canadian army. I was lucky when I met a young fellow of Norwegian descent who could speak some German. He became my guardian angel on the train to Edmonton, where we were outfitted, and back again to Grande Prairie for our basic infantry training.

I still remember, very vividly, lying on my bunk in the Edmonton Armories listening to the conversations going on around me. I did not understand much, but I noticed certain words were repeatedly used when a corporal or sergeant was mentioned, or when going to a movie, beer parlor, or payday were discussed. My friend was not in the barracks at the time, and I could hardly wait to see him. As soon as he came in, I asked him about the words I had heard. Grinning, he told me that from then on I should be very careful not to fall into the habit of using those expressions.

I gradually learned to speak by picking up word after word, and using these words to form sentences. After I received my first army pay, I started going to cheap movie matinees on Saturdays; not to see the movie, but to listen carefully to the English conversation. It helped quite a lot in adding words to my vocabulary.

I was very uncertain about my English at that time. In the mornings, when our training group lined up for inspection, I always tried to get into the center or rear rank. I was afraid the inspecting officer would stop in front of me and ask me some questions, which, with my lack of English, I was not sure I could answer, and that would have made me feel embarrassed. After two months of basic infantry training in Grande Prairie, our platoon was sent to Currie Barracks in Calgary, for advanced training. By that time, I had lost some of my shyness and frequently ended up in the front rank at inspection time.

About two weeks before my advanced training was finished, I was called into the company commander's office. Captain Tucker told me he wanted me to take an instructors course in small arms. I protested that I could not speak English well enough to become an instructor. He said instructors were needed, that I was learning fast, and that after six weeks in instructor training my English would be good enough. It was no use to say another word. After six weeks instructor training, and three weeks more in the instructor's school to improve my English, I was promoted to Lance Corporal and became a small arms instructor at the Advanced Infantry Training Center Currie Barracks, Calgary.

Our problems with language often involved us in some memorable incidents. The following are some stories I recall about the settlers, the language, and the various methods of overcoming the problems encountered.

What can a housewife do, if she wants to buy a candle in a

store in town, but does not know the English word to tell the clerk what she wants? That happened to Mrs. F. one day, when she went to Dawson Creek. She believed in the old saying....... where there is a will there is a way. Mrs. F. found the solution to her problem by indicating with her hands the size of candle, then making the motion of lighting it, and then blowing it out. That was the moment. The sales clerk understood, and smiled sweetly at Mrs. F..., brought some candles to the counter for her to make her choice. Mrs. F. selected some, paid for them and walked out of the store with a feeling of pride at having been able to make a purchase without speaking a word....

The homesteaders in the surrounding area were generally very friendly, helpful people. When they drove along one of our dirt roads, they always offered rides. That custom became our custom. There was one settler among us who had special hauling to do and thus was the first one to be assigned his own team and wagon.

One day he, I shall call him Josef Fleischer, was on his way to look for some hens he wanted to buy. Along the trail he overtook a man walking in the same direction. Josef thought that this man was one of the neighboring homesteaders, who would know where some laying hens could be bought. But the conversation between the driver and his passenger was rather scant, since the passenger just shrugged his shoulders when Josef started to speak. Fleischer thought his lousy English might be the cause of his passenger's actions, but he wanted to know where he could buy laying hens, so he tried again. It did not work; his passenger again shrugged his shoulders and said nothing.

Determined to make himself understood, Fleischer made flying movements with his arms and shouted, "caca-ca-ca-cacaca-ca. cacaca-caca," imitating a hen after she had laid an egg. The face of his passenger then brightened and smiling he said: "Ach Hayner meanst Du?" (Oh, you mean hens?). That response got the conversation going.....Josef's passenger turned out to be another Sudeten settler heading for the same place for the same purpose.

Sometimes sign language backfired, as Rudi P. found out when he had a bad itch in his throat and needed a remedy.

Rudi went to the drug store in Dawson Creek to get

something for the miserable itch. He could not explain to the druggist what his trouble was or what he wanted and got more nervous every minute trying to remember some English words. But none came to him.

When Rudi got nervous he had the habit of scratching his head. The druggist must have thought: "a ha, that guy must have trouble with lice." He went to the shelf and brought Rudi a louse powder, which Rudi later took with a glass of water. Rudi is still around, but whether that louse powder did the trick in curing the itch in his throat, I never found out. Thank goodness this mistake did not cause more serious trouble for our friend.

Paul L., whom everyone in the settlement knew for his language blunders when he went to town to buy something, went to town one day to buy a pitman for his binder. Somehow he managed to get the part all right, but when he got home he found it did not fit the shaft of the binder. The hole was not big enough.

When he went back to the dealer the next day, Paul could not remember the English word "small". Thus, he pointed at the hole in the part and said: "The hole is too 'KLIEN'. The dealer replied: "The hole has to be clean, it is a new part you know." "Yes", said Paul, "I know, but the hole it too 'Klien'," and pointed again at the hole in the pitman. Because the sound of Paul's German word for **small** was like the English word **clean** the dealer was understandably confused.

How Paul and the dealer finally understood each other I do not know. I understand Paul's binder worked again, so he must have received help from someone to straighten things out.

Our native language sometimes played tricks on us when we thought we were the only ones who understood.

Resl, a well-liked plump lady, went to Dawson Creek one day, with a friend, to buy herself a chamber pot. After she purchased her chamber pot, she carefully carried her package on to the bus for the trip back home. Not far from the two women sat a man who was as well-rounded out as Resl. When Resl spotted the man, she said in German to her friend, "I bet you the fat a....of that man would not fit on my chamber pot." The fat man heard her and said in even better German, "And I bet you, yours won't fit either."

Sometimes the English words we did learn and use, were the wrong words at the wrong time, or in the wrong company. It can be embarrassing if one uses the wrong words in the wrong company.

W.D...., one of our horsemen, offered a ride to the Roman Catholic Priest, Father Owen, one day. His horses did not please W. D. for some reason, so he did what many a horse driver has done. He swore at the horses in the best English he could master. Father Owen said, "You can speak good English, my son, but bad, bad, bad words."

14

WOMEN AND WORK

Much of the success of our farms was due to the work of the women. The old saying that behind every good man there is a woman, was proven over and over again, during the establishment of the Sudeten German settlement. The women worked in the fields beside their husbands, cared for the vegetable gardens and livestock as well as caring for their children and performing household chores. They too, had to learn new skills. When their husbands went away to work for other farmers, on the Alaska highway, or on construction projects in Dawson Creek, the women carried on the farming operation.

The following excerpt from an article which appeared in the **Edmonton Journal** in August 1939 gives some idea of the first experiences of the women after they arrived in the settlement.

"One of the most prominent residents of the Tupper B.C. Sudeten refugee settlements is mop-haired, pipe-smoking Dr. Arnold Glass whose deft fingers once performed a half dozen appendectomies every day in a Prague hospital and who now had learned to handle a hammer, a saw, a planer......Mrs. Glass has worked in the fields and has learned to milk. One could appreciate the situation if a well-to-do Edmonton medical man and his wife suddenly were ordered out to a farm there to lead a farming life.

"But Dr. Glass and Mrs. Glass don't mind. Mrs. Glass, who once was a milliner, said proudly, "where my husband goes, I go too." And they like Canada. "Here there is enough to eat," said Dr. Glass.

"When I visited the camp I arrived in the middle of a red letter day. The women had spent the morning picking peas until they had a huge green mound.....

"Dr. Glass and his wife had peas for their dinner that evening, and Mrs. Glass was particularly proud that she had a hand in keeping the pea garden clean of weeds."

Mrs. Glass, like many other women, had learned to milk while the cows were tied to trees or in a small corral before barns were built. Her white shorts and those of other women, customary dress for summer work in the old country, attracted a good deal of attention from the passengers on the trains passing through Tupper station four times each week. The grove of trees and corrals were located close to the station, and the women were easily seen. The train conductors knew many of their passengers and often pointed out the sights which could be seen.

After we were moved to our own farms, the women continued to use their new skills. Many men worked outside the settlement to provide a livelihood for their families and a cash income with which to buy much needed livestock and equipment. That could not have been done without the women. The wives often had to take full responsibility for the work around the farms. Men who worked in Dawson Creek and could come home on weekends did. But what could he accomplish in little more than one day? Perhaps he could cut some firewood for the cast iron cook stove, or stoke the sheet metal heater. That would relieve his wife of one never ending chore.

While their husbands were away during winter, some women had to haul water a distance of up to six miles. If the small dugout was frozen, the little water left under the thick ice was of such an evil smell that neither beast nor man could use it. If there was enough snow on the ground, then one or two steel barrels had to be set up to melt snow for the livestock and the household.

Most of the settlers had some pigs, which required daily care. If one of the brood sows was due to farrow, the women had to watch that the sow did not squash some of the piglets. That required getting up every night, regardless of the weather or exhaustion, during the last few nights before the litter was expected. Sometimes piglets had to be bottle-fed if they were too weak to fight for the nipple on the mother sow, or if there were not enough nipples for a large litter. It was imperative that every piglet be saved, to provide some income.

The few cows in the settlement were also a source of income, but they also required a lot of care and work to produce that income. Here again, it was the women who did the milking, separated the cream and washed the equipment. When their husbands were away, they also fed the cattle, cleaned the barn, and hauled the cream to the store on shipping days. The cream was collected there for shipment by rail to Grande Prairie.

Barns were not the only thing they cleaned. The train conductors told their passengers that these new people, who had settled in the valley, even washed their chicken houses with soap and water. Whether these statements were absolutely accurate or not, our women earned their reputation for hard work. Even when their husbands were home, women often helped them picking roots and rocks, burning trash on newly broken land or hauling it away. At harvest time, women could be seen walking behind the horse drawn binders, stooking the sheaves of cut grain. In some cases they operated the binder and stooked the sheaves afterward, with the help of their children.

The women of the settlement often suffered most from their lack of English and the opportunity to learn it. Children learned English in school, while men learned it by a variety of methods, but the women had fewer opportunities. Their trips to town were few. They had little contact with English speaking neighbors or the settlement supervisors. Therefore few of them picked up new words as their husbands and children did.

My wife also experienced many of these hardships during the winter of 1940/41 and while I was in the Canadian army.

During our first season on our own farm we could not become self-sustaining and had been given credit by the land settlement company. The company owned and operated a lumber camp in which settlers provided the labor. I cannot remember the wages paid because it was not paid in cash, but credited to our settler account. Besides the wages, each settler was to receive 200 board feet of lumber.

When I was told that I had been detailed for two weeks work in the lumber camp in February of 1941, I could not refuse. I was indebted to the company, needed the lumber for building, and I felt the offer carried with it the implication that our credit might be cut off, so I went. I still remember, very clearly, that those two weeks work in the lumber did not make a big dent in my debit account.

The camp accommodation was primitive. Those who slept in the upper bunks were too hot; those in the lower bunks, too cold. There was no regulator on the sheet metal heater, which burned all day long. Pack rats and squirrels tunneled their way through the moss-filled cracks in the log walls. They became a great nuisance at night with their chattering, and were sometimes shot with .22 rifles some of the men brought to the camp. Mice also found their way in, but we seldom heard them at night. We were tired and slept.

The women of the settlement also became inventive as they tried to solve household problems, or provide treats for their families and friends. Sometimes their attempts resulted in humorous incidents, like the making of fly catchers.

Flies and mosquitos were constant tormentors of the settlers. One day, Grete L..., after looking at the lumps from mosquito bites on her arms and neck, decided to make some fly catchers. She remembered the old type fly catchers as only strips of paper with some honey on them. There was some wrapping paper in the house, so she cut it in strips. There was no honey in the house so she decided to use syrup. "Nothing to it", she said to a friend, as she dipped the paper strips in the syrup. In the heat, the syrup ran all over the place, leaving her "fly catchers" as naked as a baby's bottom. The wicked mosquitos and flies continued to bite her as furiously as they had before.

Another time, I recall the women of the Springhill group making beer. The first batch did not work out too well.

After malting barley became available, and someone had found out that hops could be bought in the Dawson Creek Co-op store, the women of the Springhill group decided to brew some beer as a change from the poor drinking water.

Bottles had been collected along the highway for a long time. Finally there were enough and the first experiment in brewing began. Everything seemed to go as expected. The brew looked like beer and smelled like beer. After filling, the bottles were put in the coolest place which could be found.

But a few days later: Bang! Bang! Bang! It sounded like an enemy army was approaching Springhill and was starting to soften up that fortress with heavy artillery, before a frontal attack could be started.

When the frightened ladies looked, after the first shock had worn off, they found that most of their bottles had exploded. Their first experiment in brewing beer had ended in a complete failure. But after that, they knew what they had done wrong: bottling the brew too soon was the cause of the explosions. Other bottles were collected and another beer brew followed, which was a smashing success.

The women of the settlement learned new skills, and experimented to try to overcome the primitive conditions. Women were often the key to success on the farms and often did a man's job.

15
TIME OUT FROM WORK

Our first community dances were held in the schoolhouse. After the log community hall was built we held dances and celebrated traditional festivals there. Practical jokes were sometimes played on people while they were working. Although not always appreciated by the victims, these were a break in the work routine. Families also celebrated traditional festivals in their own homes and visited their neighbors.

Our harvests during the first years were nothing to be excited about, but that did not prevent us from having harvest festivals. The walls of the hall were decorated with sheaves of grain. Grapes and other fruits were hung from the ceiling. The fruit was needed for a game we played. Fruit was stolen by a thief, who was then arrested by a policeman and turned over to a stern judge who fined the thief. It was great fun, and the fines helped to pay for improvements to the community hall. At this festival we also danced to music by talented members of the group.

At Christmas the entire community turned out to celebrate. We celebrated Christmas Eve the way we had in our former homeland. For that occasion, a large spruce tree was brought into the hall and decorated with painted pine cones, tinsel, glass ornaments and candles. Old German Christmas songs were sung, accompanied on the piano by Mrs. Jhonny Neubauer, a young school teacher who had married one of the settlers. The atmosphere created was always nostalgic, as we remembered the friends and loved ones we had had to leave behind.

Again, on New Years Eve, nearly everyone came to the community hall to celebrate. Hubert Leinsmer, a former newspaperman, usually compiled all the happenings during the year in the settlement into witty verses which formed the entertainment for the evening. Some people sometimes took the kidding the wrong way but it was generally meant to entertain not to make people angry. Music for dancing was provided by the Kreuzinger family. Joseph Kreuzinger had worked in a musical instrument factory, and was a skilled musician on brass instruments and the violin. His sons, Walter and Arnold, followed in their father's footsteps and became good musicians.

Our dances and festivals were often crowded as friends and visitors for miles around joined in the fun. Many times there were so many people in the hall that there was little room for dancing. The women in the community, who always brought cakes and pastries to these gatherings, sometimes had difficulty serving lunch to such large crowds.

For sometime there was a Glee Club in the settlement which put on programs in the community hall. But our settlement was small, and as people moved away others with voices needed for good harmony could not be found. Eventually the Club disbanded.

There were among the group, as with any group, a few practical jokers. Their jokes gave us the opportunity to laugh at ourselves, about our inexperience, fears, and ambitions.

One of the settlers, known as the professor, was detailed to work the midnight shift on the Caterpillar tractor during the early years of the settlement, when land breaking went on around the clock. One of the jokers among the breaking crew unhitched the plow from the tractor just before the professor took the wheel, and hid in the bush. The professor, inexperienced in this type of work, climbed onto the tractor and took off without noticing that he had no plow behind him. When he came around to the place he had started from, he saw a plow sitting in the field. He stopped and began to swear about the fool who had left a plow in his way.

The fellow, who was hidden in the bush, came out of his hiding place and asked the excited professor what the trouble was. The professor swore some more and declared he was not going to move the plow. After listening for a while to the angry outbursts, the practical joker said "Why not look behind you?" The professor did, and was surprised that the plow in front was the one which should have been behind him. Then the practical joker helped hitch the plow to the tractor, calming the nervous professor enough to carry on.

Several of the settlers were afraid of the wild animals they might encounter. With experience in the bush country, they soon realized they had little to fear despite the unverified stories which some believed. The only real threat to the people of the settlement were black bears with young cubs — in case someone came upon them unexpectedly.

Again, it was the professor working the night shift, breaking land, who was the victim. It was known that he was not very eager to meet one of the bears he had heard so much about. Karl Ritschel, a lively fun-loving fellow, could not resist the urge to play a joke on the professor. Before the professor went to work one dark windy night, Karl told him some gruesome stories about what bears could do to unsuspecting humans out alone in the dark — just to warm him up. Later, when he heard the tractor stop for lunch break, he sneaked up behind the professor, who was sitting near the tractor eating. Karl jumped out of the darkness at the professor with the best bear growl he could master. The shocked professor didn't even realize that the bear hadn't scratched him or that it had no claws. When he recovered from the shock, he gave Karl a well-deserved tongue lashing. I understand it was some time before the professor forgave Karl.

Our meager standard of living in the rough raw bushland often lead us to dream of better things. These dreams sometimes created unwary victims for practical jokers.

While unsuccessfully drilling for water on land where the Northwest group lived, the drill bit brought up odd looking pieces of material. One day some glittering yellowish bits of rock came up. These caught the eye of my drilling companion, whom I shall call H.L. He picked up pieces of the rock and put them in his pocket.

I learned later that H.L. had taken these rocks to one of the young settlers who had been a university student. The former student was known to us as very knowledgeable but also ready for a good joke. He looked the rocks over, pretended great interest in them, and said he was fairly certain they contained gold.

Through the next few days, the drilling crew noticed that H.L. watched like a hawk what came out of the hole. One day he told us he had to go to the ranch where the settlement office was located. We found out later that he had gone to the settlement supervisor intending to stake his claim on the quarter section where we were drilling. He thought he would strike it rich if he could settle on that land. He was told that nobody could claim any land at that time.

Our friend and drilling companion lost nothing by not getting that quarter section. What he had held in his hands and had so carefully put in his pockets was fools' gold, which had made a fool out of him.

I cannot recall how the next get-rich-quick scheme started, but I admit I had a share in it after I heard a rumor one Sunday in the early spring of 1940.

The rumor was that signs of oil had been found on section twenty-four. I knew that section well, because I had many times wandered over it hunting rabbits and prairie chicken. I had seen oily spots in the many small sloughs, but never in my wildest imagination had I thought that these spots were signs of oil in the ground. A number of people did believe that, and asked my opinion when they learned I was familiar with that particular piece of land. I did not like the motives of these people, but instead of discounting their claims, I encouraged them.

Sure enough on a Sunday morning shortly after they had talked to me, I watched about fifteen men walking by my shack on their way to that promising section. It was late in the evening when I saw them stumbling along on their way home. They still had about six miles to go when I saw them. They must have walked about twenty-five miles that day through a new layer of deep snow. I never heard that oil rumor again.

Sometimes neighbors and friends gathered in smaller groups. An empty house on Valentin Dittrich's land, which served as a temporary meeting place for the C.C.F. group, was also the social center for this group. We sometimes gathered there to play cards and visit. The Roman Catholic priest, Father Goetz, who enjoyed playing cards and seldom missed card parties, was with us one night when he played a trick on Alois Seitner.

Father Goetz realized that most of the settlers were not particularly religious after the experiences they had had. He sometimes teased us about that. On this particular night Father Goetz said to his card game friend, "I'll bet you a round of beer, Alois, that you can't say the Lord's Prayer". Alois replied, "I bet you Father Goetz that you are the one who has to pay for the round of beer," and started to say the prayer. Alois did not go far beyond "Our Father which art in Heaven . . .," when he started to stutter and then stopped. Alois knew he had been beaten and took out his wallet to pay for the round. Everyone laughed and drank their beer with great delight, especially Father Goetz.

One family celebration of Christmas remains in my memory because it was the day after the threshing of our disasterous crop in 1941. It had started to snow while I was on my way home Christmas Eve. The next morning it was very cold and dreary, and the snow must have been more than a foot deep. The frost on the windows of our shack formed some of winter's nicest art. Toward midday the sun came through the heavy clouds and I ventured out to look for a Christmas tree. I found a pine tree after wandering around for some time in the deep snow. After setting it up in the shack, we decorated it with pine cones painted silver, gold, papier mache ornaments, and some cookies. It was not a Christmas in splendor, but it was a Christmas in peace.

There was little community social life during the war years because many had left the settlement for industrial work in eastern Canada or joined the Canadian army. After the war, a wider variety of entertainment became available within the settlement. Better roads and transportation meant that we could go to movies and entertainment in Dawson Creek. The political differences within the community also changed our social life. During the early years of the settlement, however, dances, practical jokes and family celebrations broke the cycle of work and sleep before we could determine our own schedules on our own farms. After we moved to separate farms, the social gatherings gave us the chance to visit with friends from other parts of the settlement. A break from work was always enjoyable.

16
VISITORS AND NEIGHBORS

The settlers contact with native Canadians was infrequent because of the long hours of work and poor roads. However, the Sudeten settlement had many visitors, particularly during the first stage of its development. News reporters came to see and interview the new settlers; agriculturalists came to see for themselves how inexperienced people were getting on in their new endeavour. Nearby neighbors became friends with some of the settlers and sometimes visited the settlement. We also became familiar with the towns of Dawson Creek and Pouce Coupe.

The most distinguished visitors were two Canadian governors-general. His Excellency, Lord Tweedsmuir, came on August 17, 1939, shortly after the arrival of the last transport of settlers to the settlement. His successor, the Earl of Athlone, visited the settlement in April 1941.

The following is an excerpt from the **Edmonton Journal** of August 18, 1939, which describes the visit by Lord Tweedsmuir. The headline read: "500 Refugees Voice Welcome to Governor. Homes of Sudetens Decorated with Spruce Boughs for Occasion. Arches of Welcome. Now Free People in Free Country. They Tell Lord Tweedsmuir."

"Canada's governor-general received homage Thursday from smiling and applauding refugees from Czechoslovakia, heard them report proudly that ' we as free people have found a new home here in a free country ', and warmly welcomed them to the dominion in the name of his Majesty the King.

"The mutual greeting and the ceremonies linked with it formed a vivid highlight of Lord Tweedsmuir's tour over N.A.R. lines through northern Alberta and the Peace River block of B.C.

"The governor's reception by the ex-refugees took place on the Gundy ranch near this point, 472 miles northwest of

Edmonton, late Thursday afternoon. Five hundred Sudetens have settled here and are rebuilding their lives as farmers since Hitler swallowed their homeland last year.

"Lord Tweedsmuir showed lively interest in all details of the Sudetens dramatic story of escape from harried Europe to the new world of peace and freedom.

"The colonists presented him with an album of photographs and an address of welcome, written in flawless English. All the cabins and other buildings in the settlement were gaily garbed with spruce boughs, and welcoming arches had been erected at the entrances. The colonists cheered and applauded when Lady Tweedsmuir distributed candy among the Sudeten children.

"Lord Tweedsmuir obviously was stirred by the warmth of his welcome. In a firm voice, he wished the settlers "Every happiness and prosperity."

"All through their history, Britain and her dominions have been glad to give homes to exiles who had honorably left their own countries," he declared.

" 'Canada can give you a great deal, but there is also a good deal that you can give to Canada", the governor told them, his remarks being translated into German as soon as he had finished. He exhorted the Sudetens to maintain their old traditions, but to be good Canadians too.

"Autos from Pouce Coupe and Dawson Creek met the vice-regal party when it arrived at Tupper and escorted the governor and his suite to the settlement at Gundy ranch.

"Lord Tweedsmuir walked over a large field of newly-broken land and watched settlers pulling stumps. The men were stripped to the waist, tanned as brown as walnuts.

"Traveling later over a pond near the Pouce Coupe river, the governor's car became stuck in the mud and had to be towed out. Other cars met a similar fate. Lord Tweedsmuir grinned broadly and appeared to enjoy the experience."

The Earl of Athlone's car suffered a similar fate when he visited the settlement in 1941. After the formalities of the welcome celebrations and speeches were over, the governor-general wanted to see more of the settlement than the few buildings around the settlement office and school house. He decided that he wanted to see some of the newly established farmsteads east of there. In order to reach those farmsteads Tupper Creek had to be crossed. Everything went just fine until the creek crossing. The water in the creek was a little higher than usual and when the car was almost through, it got stuck. Settlers, who had followed the car, went into the creek in their high rubber boots and tried to push it out. But it was of no use. The rear wheels spun and would not get hold. Horses and chains had to be fetched from a nearby farmstead to pull the car out of the creek. I do not know if the Earl had ever had an experience like that before, but I recall he took it jokingly.

After some visits to farmsteads, the governor-general was honored guest at a banquet in the log community hall. I remember the settlers sang "Home, home on the range", as part of the entertainment. I have often wondered what the Earl may have written in his diary about our singing.

The Earl of Athlone's visit also provided an example of how the settlers handled their transportation problem. This particular example also gave entertainment to the crowd waiting for the governor-general to arrive.

The scheduled time of arrival of the governor-general had passed, but there still was no car in sight, as far as one could see down the highway. With every black car that came along, the excitement of the waiting crowd and the nervousness of the speaker assigned to give the welcoming address, increased. Finally, a large black limousine was seen approaching and somebody announced that this must be the expected distinguished visitor. The limousine slowed down as it came close to the assembled crowd and stopped. As the door opened, so opened the mouth of the speaker, but just in time he closed it again, as out stepped Resl Kopp. She lived near the highway and was in the habit of catching rides with passersby whenever she wanted to go somewhere. A wave of laughter went through the crowd, easing the excitement and nervousness. The governor-general arrived a few minutes later.

My first visit to a nearby farmer's home came shortly after we had moved to the Northwest group settlement. We all longed for fresh vegetables and had heard that a homesteader, living not far away, had vegetables he was willing to sell. A friend, who had lived in England and was more proficient in English than I, joined me for our first visit to this homesteader.

This was the first of many visits I made to see Angus Bell.

He was an unfaltering optimist. Angus told us he had worked as a C.P.R. train conductor in Manitoba; that he had developed stomach trouble, and decided to give up his job and regain his health as a homesteader. His family, he said, wanted no part of homesteading and had stayed in Manitoba. I thought that a man who decided, of his own free will, to go into the bush country to take up homesteading, must, by nature, not only have lots of guts but also must be an optimist.

We had come to the area in groups. We lived in groups and worked in groups the first year. Even after we moved to our assigned quarter sections, neighbors were not more than a half a mile or a mile apart. To live and work alone like Angus Bell was beyond our understanding.

He told us how he had built his own log house and livestock shelter, alone, before winter set in the first year. He told us his main source of income was from the sale of eggs from about two hundred chickens. Bell told us that it was a two day trip to Dawson Creek or Pouce Coupe to sell his eggs, do his shopping and haul back the materials he needed to finish his log house inside. He told us how a small vegetable plot the first year had stretched his few dollars, until he had an income from his livestock, and how it had given him some variety in his diet.

During the first three winters, when not very much could be done outside, I often went up that bush trail to visit Angus. My English was very poor but we always seemed to understand each other. He was a strict religious man, though not a church going man, who used to say, "I am a servant of the Lord. If the Lord wants me to get my hay in, there will be days for it. But if I can't get my hay in I shall not do it on a Sunday, the day of the Lord." I recall he threatened to shoot Alois Scholz who went to Bell's homestead one Sunday to get some lumber sawn to rebuild his burned down house. Scholz got his lumber sawn another day and Angus was as gentle toward him as before the incident.

His pride and joy was the circular saw he had mounted on a frame he built himself. It sometimes did not function properly. When that happened he would spend many hours, sometimes even days, to set things right. The saw was often broken down. A less even-tempered man could not have stood it without swearing like a trooper. But Angus Bell's only swear word was "son of a gun".

His saw almost caused his death. Willi Wanka expected Angus for dinner one day, but he did not show up. Wanka went over to Bell's place, but he was not in his house. Calling him did not bring an answer. Looking around Wanka found him lying beside his saw, bleeding from a head wound. He took Angus to the hospital, where he recovered, but he soon decided to give up his homestead and move to Vancouver.

Besides being a strict religious man, Angus was also well-read and something of a philosopher and dreamer. I remember him expressing the opinion that more people, like ourselves, should be brought into Canada to develop the vast areas of land suitable for agriculture, and that the resources of the country should not be sold in their raw state, but should be processed here in Canada and sold on the world market as finished goods. That, he believed, would give many more people a livelihood and would develop our road system and railroads, since more would be paying taxes and therefore help to pay for them. This would make it more convenient for people to live in this great country.

Angus Bell was very pleased that the establishing of our Sudeten settlement had brought so many new people into this sparsely settled area. There was always someone coming by his place with whom he could talk and also trade. I learned a lot from Angus and I have never forgotten what an inspiration he was to us; always a helpful neighbor. He was a dear friend and advisor to me during the early years of my trying to become a farmer. He was, I think, one of the finest human beings I ever met.

Our contact with the neighboring towns resulted from our needs for doctors, dentists, drugstores, farm machinery dealers, goods not carried in the company store and other small businesses, which make up the economy of a small town.

When the Sudeten settlers arrived, Dawson Creek and Pouce Coupe had populations of 700 and 200, respectively. Our settlement, with a population of over 500 people, made a considerable impact on these towns. Dawson Creek, in particular, played an important role in the development of our settlement. In 1932, Dawson Creek had become the railhead of the Northern Alberta Railway. There were seven grain elevators in the town, making it one of the largest grain shipping centers in the Canadian northwest.

My first visit to Dawson Creek was in the early spring of 1940. Mr. McArton, one of our supervisors, took me to Rolla to buy a cow. We stopped in Dawson Creek where he attended to some business. I had to wait about an hour for him and that gave me time to take a good look at the town I had heard so much about, but had never had a chance to see.

The main street was then just as wide as it is now, but it was just a dirt street, muddy like any other road in spring. I crossed the street, but when I was about in the middle I got stuck. The mud was so sticky and deep that it pulled off my high rubber boot as I tried to walk. There was nothing I could do but pull my boots out with my hands and walk the rest of the way across in my socks. I cleaned my feet and socks on some dry grass, put the socks on and slid my feet back into my rubber boots.

Most of the buildings in town at that time were of the kind one still sees in western movies. Many of them disappeared in an explosion in a warehouse during the construction of the Alaska highway. The explosion destroyed a large part of the inner section of the town. New buildings had replaced the old when I passed through Dawson Creek on leave from the army in the spring of 1943.

The building of the Alaska highway gave Dawson Creek the impetus it needed for further development. It became the gateway to the North because it was mile zero on the 1500 mile long highway to Fairbanks, Alaska, and had a business radius of over 100 miles.

The milk processing plant in Dawson Creek became an important factor in the economy of the Sudeten settlement. Milk and cream became sources of income for the settlers very early in the development of the settlement.

Distinguished visitors, friendly neighbors and neighboring towns all played a role in helping the Sudeten settlers become familiar with their new homeland.

17
CHANGES THROUGH TIME

Over the nearly forty years since we Sudeten Germans were settled in the Peace River district, many changes have been made in the landscape, the community, and our lives. These changes have come with increased prosperity and better transportation. The things which could not be changed were made more bearable as we prospered, but remained for me, an undesirable aspect of our home in freedom.

We were not the first people who had settled in the area. Veterans of World War I had tried to put down roots on the wooded hillsides. When we arrived, all that was left of their hopes and dreams were rotten logs of broken down cabins and traces in the bush of their attempts to cultivate the land. Today, these hillsides are almost as wooded as when the first explorers saw them. The difference is that most of trees of commercial value have been harvested, and there are some open spaces where the land is cultivated. The valley below, once covered with white and black poplar trees, willows, swamp spruce, and dotted with sloughs and muskeg, now is farmland. It is dotted with meadows, grain fields, and farmsteads. The wild animals, which were real and imagined threats to us, have been reduced by land clearing and indiscriminate hunting. The moose and deer which had trampled or eaten my hay in 1941 are rarely seen any more. The same is true of the black bears.

The hungry mosquitos which had plagued us in the early years are now almost gone. Landclearing and the drying up of sloughs and muskeg have deprived these insects of their favored breeding ground. Those which still torture people with their bites can be controlled now with repellants, an item unknown and unaffordable in the early days.

The cold winter climate, which was so unbearable to many of us at first, has not changed. Instead, we were gradually able to purchase warmer clothing to protect ourselves. It was after I returned to the settlement following World War II that I finally could afford warm boots for winter. I replaced the rags and rubber boots with a pair of fur lined overshoes to wear over moccasins and woolen socks. Only then did I feel that I could stand the low temperatures without having to perform an Indian dance or let the northern winter triumph over me. The hated parkas were worn out by then and we looked more like individuals, not like members of a clan — particularly not like the one we so much despised.

The fierce blizzards of winters past, which had prevented us from leaving our homes, continued and brought tragedy to our community in 1951. A blizzard during the first weekend in March of that year was the worst recorded in more than three decades of the district's history. Strong, gusty, forty mile per hour winds drove the chill factor of the thirty below temperature to ninety, the danger range on weather charts. The highway, from Edmonton to Dawson Creek, was heavy with drifting snow, delaying the traffic for several hours.

Mrs. Anna Wiesner, who had gone to Edmonton for a medical examination, was expected on the bus, which should have reached the settlement early Sunday evening. Her husband, Herbert, had wrapped himself up against the cold. He had taken extra blankets along when he drove his team and sleigh to the junction where he expected his wife to get off the bus. After several hours waiting for the overdue bus he could no longer stand the cold and went to a nearby farm to warm up. After about four more hours of watching and waiting, he saw the lights of the bus and rushed out to the junction to pick up his wife with the team and sleigh. But she was not there. He did not think she could have started to walk home for the snow drifts made walking almost impossible. After looking around and calling her name, with only the howling wind answering, he drove home thinking she had stayed on the bus because of the horrible weather and had gone on to Dawson Creek. But Mrs. Wiesner had not gone on to Dawson Creek. She had stepped off the bus at the junction and had frozen to death before her husband reached the spot. Her husband had not seen her in the darkness and whirling snow. Next morning a settler on his way to the settlement store, with his team and sleigh, saw an uncovered hand in the snow. Shoveling away some snow, he recognized Mrs. Wiesner. Her husband, who had nearly frozen to death himself, was horrified to learn that she was not safe in Dawson Creek.

Once again we were reminded of the fears we had had about our new home. We, again, recognized the raw realities of living in a harsh climate. We could not change the climate. We could only be wary of it.

During the late 1940's, the volume of mail passing through the Co-op store made it impossible to continue this service. In 1947, Rudolf Dworsky and Max Siegert canvassed for signatures on a petition to the postal authorities in Ottawa to establish a post office in the settlement. The reply came stating that we would have a post office but must submit three names, one of which would be chosen as the name for our new service. Tate Creek headed our list. Tomslake was on the end of our list because none of us were very impressed by the lake in the area. It was much more slough than a lake. We had chose that name because nothing better sounding had come into our minds.

Sometime after we had submitted the list of names, we received the charter for the post office. Tomslake had been chosen as the name because there was already a Tate Creek, British Columbia and duplicate names in the same province were not allowed. Rudolf Dworsky, a veteran of World War II, became the first Postmaster and the Sudeten German settlement became a dot on the map of Canada called Tomslake.

Dworsky was unable to provide a livelihood for his family on the thirty dollars per month postmaster's wage. He worked outside the settlement during the week, while his wife looked after the post office. During the early fifties, he moved to Dawson Creek to take up work as a letter carrier. Frank Kuenzel then became post master and was also appointed justice of the peace.

The population of our settlement decreased from 518 when we first arrived to 326 after fifty-nine families and twenty-five single men left to work in industry elsewhere in Canada, before 1942. Natural increase, including the birth of a daughter to Dr. Glass and his wife, brought the population up to 362 by the end of 1942. By 1955, the settlement had grown to approximately 400 people as a result of natural increase and settler sponsorship of relatives as immigrants to Canada. As can be seen in Appendix IV, many of the original settlers have died. Others have retired in nearby Pouce Coupe or Dawson Creek, or have left the district, as I did in 1959. There were eighty-seven active farmers in 1955, but today I would estimate only fifty original settlers, or their children, remain on the land.

Some economic improvement was made by the settlers during and after World War II. The cash income from jobs on the Alaska highway, and construction work in Dawson Creek, gave settlers the opportunity to purchase more livestock and better equipment, thus improving their chance to make a livelihood farming. Grade A hog prices rose slightly after the war. Most of us were able to sell our hogs to the butchers in Dawson Creek during the fifties for sixteen and eighteen cents for a good grade animal. The highest price I ever received for a Grade A live hog was twenty-one cents a pound.

The cattle we received from the settlement were not always of the best quality and were sometimes sold as canners and cutters for between six and nine cents per pound. Even the better quality animals we raised ourselves did not always sell for high prices. The best price I ever received for a 1200 pound milk fed prime steer was $216.00, sold to the butcher in Pouce Coupe for the annual barbeque. It must have been tasty beef because every year after that the butcher asked me if I had another such steer for sale.

Production of milk for the Dawson Creek market became an important source of income for some Sudeten farmers between 1942 and 1955 (Appendix III). In a conversation with Mr. Weir, the Manager of the Northern Alberta Dairy Pool in Dawson Creek, I was told that 1955 was a peak year. Forty-five shippers, who produced and shipped 1,500,000 pounds of milk, had received over $70,000 return. Since that time, Mr. Weir told me, the number of milk shippers has decreased, but mechanization has increased production. In 1975 there were only five shippers left in Tomslake, but their production was 2,700,000 pounds of milk, with a gross return of $324,000. Things certainly have changed since I shipped milk to that plant.

The year 1954 may well be considered the most important milestone of the Sudeten settlement. After fifteen years of using coal oil lamps, electric lights were switched on and our shacks were brightly lit for the first time. This event brought back part of the civilization we had lost. The entire community rejoiced when the poles went up along the roads and the wires were stretched, carrying the invisible power to individual farmsteads.

After pressing for several years for this development, the British Columbia Power Commission had been persuaded to extend their power lines the thirteen miles from Pouce Coupe to the settlement. By that time, we had all established our credit ratings with banks and credit unions in Pouce Coupe and Dawson Creek, and could obtain loans to pay for this very important improvement.

Rural electrification meant we could retire our coal oil lamps. There was no more need to grope around in the dark morning and night to find matches in the cow or hog barn. Electric heat lamps kept newborn piglets warm during the first weeks of their lives. Heat lamps also kept water from freezing during the cold winter nights. We no longer had the tedious task of stoking the wood burning heater in garages to warm up the tractor engine so it would start. By placing two heat lamps under the tractor for a few hours it started easily, even in the coldest weather.

Electricity in the house changed things too. An electric heater was convenient during the cold winter nights. We no longer had to shiver in bed in our poorly insulated shacks when the wood burning heater needed stoking. The old battery radio, which usually had stopped working when it was most inconvenient to go to town for new batteries, could be replaced by one run on electricity.

We did not retire all our coal oil lamps. There was still need for one where electric lines did not reach, such as walking to neighbors on a dark night in late fall or winter. I recall I converted a coal oil lamp to electricity and by using an extension cord I had a mobile light.

Roads within the settlement and links to Pouce Coupe and Dawson Creek were improved after the war. With these improvements and increasing cash incomes from farming, the business of the Co-op declined. The increasing numbers of cars and pick-up trucks in the settlement made it possible to shop in Dawson Creek where a larger variety of merchandise was offered than in our small community store. The Co-op in Tomslake dissolved during the sixties because of the small number of prospective customers and several deficit years. The members transferred to the large Co-op in Dawson Creek, where many of them had been doing most of their shopping anyway.

Social life in the community changed after the war. Better roads and transportation made it possible to go outside the settlement for entertainment. New kinds of entertainment were put on in the settlement.

After the war, German movies were shown in the community hall. These were attended by those who did not understand sufficient English to follow an English language movie. Later, two truckers took movie lovers to Dawson Creek when a movie with a good rating was being shown. These trips were always lots of fun, when we all crowded into the boxes of the trucks. We nearly always met some one we had not seen for a long time. There was usually lots of kidding on these trips and our jolly Resl, who never missed one, was always teased about having to buy two seats in the theatre because she would not fit in one.

A theatre club was formed to present German plays. These performances required weeks of rehearsal and many long hours traveling for the actors and actresses. The plays were always well-attended; some were so popular that they had to be repeated. We were very proud of our amateur theatre group.

The most dramatic change in our social life came in 1953, when our log community hall burned to the ground. The fire destroyed our library as well as our meeting place. Unfortunately, the political differences which had split the community became more obvious when rebuilding the hall. The smaller group, who had abandoned some of their social democratic views, had dominated the administration of the old hall. All of the original settlers had, however, helped to build the hall, or contributed to it through their share in the settlement fund. When the fire insurance money was received by the community hall administration, they refused to grant an equal share to the larger group nor equal rights to a new hall. There are currently two new community halls in Tomslake. One belongs to the group which calls itself "Canadian German Alliance", the other belongs to the larger group who support the New Democratic Party. The latter celebrated a grand opening in May 1955.

Two community halls resulted in a need for dance music. The settler Josef Kreutzinger with his sons Walter and Arno and Walter Fischer formed the first brass band in the settlement and played for dances in the old community hall. Later a group of young people formed a modern dance band called "The Continentals", which put on a great performance at the opening ceremonies of the new NDP hall in 1955 and played mostly in this hall for dances. Jonny Neubauer, along with his wife, who had accompanied our Christmas carol singing so often, and his brother Frank, formed a dance band shortly after the minority group's hall was completed. I have danced to their music and found it most enjoyable. Jonny played the saxaphone and Frank the accordian and guitar.

The loss of the library was a serious blow to the cultural life of our community. A new library was established in one of the original framehouses, and Mrs. Alois Hilbert worked many hours cataloguing and recording the lending of the new reading material.

Valentin Dittrich donated land for a sportsfield and the young people soon gathered there to play soccer. With this the basics for recreation were available within the community and we could claim a reasonable social and cultural life.

The empty space in Dawson Creek, where I dried my muddy feet in 1940, is currently occupied by a television station. Willi Schoen, after he retired, organized a television show which was broadcast from this station. The program included good music and items on German culture. This show was widely acclaimed and made a contribution to German culture in Canada. German viewers of B.C.T.V., Dawson Creek, greatly miss this program. It was discontinued when Mr. Schoen died.

The many years of pioneer farming did not dull the Sudeten German's love of culture and entertainment. Individually, and as a group, they have tried to preserve some of the good things of German culture.

By 1967, when Canada celebrated its one hundredth anniversary of Confederation, the Sudeten settlers of Tomslake had lived almost thirty years of their lives in their new homeland. When we gathered to celebrate Canada's Centennial, many of our children had become the parents of a new generation of Canadians. Those who had come twenty-nine years before wanted to show their appreciation and love for their new homeland. They built a small park as a rest stop for tourists passing by. A plaque, in the Tomslake Centennial Park, briefly tells the story of our settlement.

TRAVELLER

In September 1938 when the prime ministers of Great Britain and France met the German and Italian dictators in Munich, they brought "peace in our time" with the surrender of the Sudetenland to the Third Reich. Part of the price paid for deceptive peace was the abadonment of the last free Germans. The thousands of Sudeten German anti-Nazis who in the face of overwhelming odds would not give up their struggle for freedom and democracy — to a fate of annihilation for some and persecution for the rest. Many were thrown into concentration camps of the Third Reich. Fortunately, however, several thousand escaped into the free western countries, with more than one thousand men, women and children being welcomed by a generous Canadian government in 1939. Half of them settled in the valley before you and on the hills around, and while the world was bent upon wholesale destruction in the years following the Munich Agreement, the people from the Sudetenland, with steadfast determination and hard work, built farmsteads here where they could rear their children as free people in a free country. At the same time 46 of their young men served in the Canadian Forces, most of them overseas.

In Canada's centennial year they erected this stopping place as a symbol of their deep gratitude to their new homeland.

18

THE ALPHA AND OMEGA

The story of the Sudeten German emigration, which began in September 1938, did not end until May 1945. The emigration was rooted in the treaties of Versailles and St. Germaine, which created new states but did not eliminate national minority problems. Instead, it created over 11,000 kilometers of new frontiers behind which the same problems continued to plague domestic and, indirectly, international relations. Inflation, economic depression, internal political struggles, and another world war between 1918 and 1945 each contributed to the final expulsion of the Sudeten Germans from Czechoslovakia.

Runaway inflation in Germany, in 1923, weakened the infant Weimar republic, which carried a very large war reparations debt imposed by the victors of World War I. Building a democratic state and rebuilding an economy on the ashes of a monarchy and a war was made more difficult by these burdens. Before the republic was firmly established, the great depression damaged the economy and created an unemployment rate nearly three times that of other western powers in 1932. The victors of World War I required that reparation payments continue according to the terms of the Versailles treaty, in spite of the economic plight of the Weimar republic.

The economic turmoil of the thirties became the spawning ground for the Nazi movement. Without the moral and financial support of other western nations, the democratic government was unable to withstand the constant criticism of democracy and government policy by the Nazis. The barons of finance and industry, the Prussian land lords, and the unemployed colonels and generals of the defunct Kaiser's army saw democratic rule as a threat to their positions of power. On January 30, 1933, with the help of a senile state president, they manipulated Adolf Hitler into power when the Nazi party did not have a majority in the Reichstag. A reign of terror within the country began almost immediately.

After internal opposition to his regime had been eliminated, Hitler began to concentrate on foreign affairs. In October 1933, Nazi Germany withdrew from the League of Nations and also from a disarmament conference. The Nazi regime then began preparations for war. The Rhineland was militarized in March 1935, in defiance of the Locarno Pact. During the same month Hitler ordered military conscription in Germany, which violated the terms of peace contained in the Treaty of Versailles. The Spanish Civil War of 1936 became the testing ground for the growing Nazi war machine. The western powers looked on with closed eyes while democracy was murdered.

When Hitler realized that the western powers had taken no action against his violations of international agreements, he became bolder. On January 30, 1937, the fourth anniversary of his diabolic regime, he repudiated the Versailles peace treaty in total, and declared Nazi Germany free of all obligations under that treaty. Thirteen months later, on March 11, 1938, Austria was invaded by Hitler's army and made a part of the Third Reich. Again, the western powers took no direct counter action. Hitler then boldly declared that the Third Reich would prevail for 1000 years. His unchecked successes made him so bold that just six months later he occupied the Sudetenland. The timing of these acts of aggression was maintained when, six months later, March 14, 1939, the remaining part of Czechoslovakia was swallowed by Nazi Germany. Part of it became a protectorate, under the rule of the Nazi protector. The province of Slovakia was declared an independent state. In reality, it was a puppet state.

Hitler's plan to control central Europe was assisted by the Communist dictator, Joseph Stalin, when he signed a ten year non-aggression pact with Nazi Germany on August 24, 1939. One week later Poland was attacked and divided between the Soviets and Hitler's Germany. The deal between these two gangsters lasted twenty-two months. Hitler's armies invaded the Soviet Union on June 22, 1941, and the worst holocaust in history began.

In his megalomania Hitler declared war on the United States on December 11, 1941. I listened to his speech that day on the radio in Canada. I still can hear his screeching voice when he said, "Und wenn der Herr Roosevelt zu feige ist den Krieg zu erklaeren, dann erklaere ich den Krieg ." (And if Mr. Roosevelt is too cowardly to declare war, then I declare war.) He even pronounced the name Roosevelt in such a way that it was given a Jewish tinge.

That day, in December 1941, was the first time since the Munich debacle that hope for the rebirth of freedom and democracy in Europe dawned in me. I recall I went to my neighbor after Hitler's speech ended and happily asked him, "Do you realize what happened today?" He did not understand my joy so I declared, "Nazi Germany lost the war today. Europe and our homeland will soon be free again."

I was only partly right. When the war finally ended in May 1945, our homeland was lost to our people. Joseph Stalin had his way in Potsdam, when the western powers agreed to the expulsion of three and one-half million Sudeten Germans from their homeland. Regrettably, British Prime Minister Clement Attlee, who had championed the cause of our political refugees in 1939, forgot all the good he had done and signed the Potsdam agreement. The Sudeten German people were driven from a homeland they had built, lived and worked in for over 800 years.

Even before the Potsdam agreement was signed, in August 1945, notices like the following were posted in the Sudentenland:

"The inhabitants of German nationality residing in the municipalities of Boehmisch Leipa, Alt Leipa, and Niemens, irrespective of age and sex, will leave their lodgings on June 15th, 1945 at 5 a.m.

"Each individual to whom this expulsion order refers may take with him provisions for seven days plus personal necessities not in excess of what one person is able to carry.

"Objects to be handed over at the collection point are the following: gold, silver, and any objects made of such metals, bank deposit books, insurance policies, cash, except for 100 Reichmark per person, and cameras.

"This notice serves as a warning that all will be subjected to severe body search. Concealment of any of the above mentioned objects either in one's clothing, shoes or other places, such as hand luggage and the like, is therefore to no avail and will be severely punished.

Boehmisch Leipa the 14th of June 1946
Local Military Commandant
(Signed) pplk Voves"

These cruel notices chased the Sudeten Germans over the borders of Czechoslovakia with about twenty-five kilograms of their earthly goods with them. This genocidal expulsion caused the death of thousands. Some died on the march out of their homeland. There were many reports that others were slain by the Czechs or died in Czech concentration camps. These people had to pay for the sins of Nazism whether they had sided with the Nazis or had been vehemently opposed to Nazism. The wrong which had been done by Nazi Germany was replaced by an even greater wrong.

The instigators of this wrong did not derive many happy hours from their deeds. Less than three years later Czechoslovakia, which had been a free country after the war, fell victim to another dictatorship. The Czech Communist Party, with the backing of the Soviet Union, took control of the country. Dr. Eduard Beneš, whose conspiracy with Joseph Stalin had led to the expulsion of the Sudeten Germans, was replaced by Klement Gottwald, as president of Czechoslovakia. The Foreign Minister, Jan Masaryk, who lacked the greatness of his father, the first president of the Czechoslovak republic, mysteriously found his death by a fall out of the window of his office.

Out of the ashes and debris of the Third Reich a new Germany was born. The millions of refugees who had flooded in found a new home and a livelihood there in spite of the many obstacles they had to overcome. Today, approximately twenty percent of the population of West Germany are those who were forced to leave their homelands.

Many thousands of anti-Nazi Germans, who succeeded in escaping Nazi persecution, have found homes in free countries all over the world. They have stayed there long after the thousand year Reich of Adolf Hitler found its deserved end, after twelve years of bloody existence.

In Canada, a respectable number of Sudeten German refugees established settlements in British Columbia and Saskatchewan. Many served their new homeland in the Canadian army. Others left the settlements to take up work in the cities, because a livelihood could not be made in these settlements. Those who left have proven successful in many fields of endeavour. Most of the settlers who remained on their farmsteads are now retired and living in towns or cities where they can enjoy the many conveniences they missed during their lives as pioneer farmers. The compensation payments given them by the new democratic West Germany for losses sustained during the Nazi regime have helped to make this possible. Their farmsteads have been taken over by their children, sold, or leased to a neighbor or a newcomer. The farming communities they built still contribute to the agricultural production of Canada, as the world strives to feed the hungry.

In West Germany I have visited similar communities of Sudeten Germans. On a hillside near Stuttgart stands a beautiful section of a city where once there were only tree stumps and a lonely sightseeing tower. Its name is Stumpenhof, part of the city of Plochingen. Deep in Bavaria, there is a thriving community called New Gablonz, in the city of Kaufbeuren. The glass artists of old Gablonz lost their material goods when they were driven from their homes, but no one could take away their world renowned skill. They went to Bavaria, and have given West Germany a new industry. The glass factory they built now competes in the world market with the old plant in Czechoslovakia. It plays an important role in the export trade of West Germany.

An old friend of mine, who lives with her family in Rosenheim, Bavaria, wrote the following in a letter to me:

"We also have in our area settlements like Tomslake, of which we are very proud. They are Wald-Kraiburg and Traunreuth in the county of Traunreuth. Both are in the middle of a forest where, under the Nazi regime, there were underground bunkers. The Sudeten Germans, other German refugees, and expatriates have converted these bunkers into industrial enterprises. Wald-Kraiburg is now a beautiful city of about

25,000 people, with a former inhabitant of Freiwaldauin the Sudentenland as mayor. Traunreuth has also developed into an important industrial community, with a large Siemans household appliance plant as the main employer."

Tomslake, like other settlements in Canada and West Germany, is the symbol of many Sudeten German defeats. It is also one of our triumphs.

APPENDIX I

Financial Statements and Map

The following is a summary of Assets of the Tate Creek Development Company, as of January 12, 1943, when the board of directors elected by the settlers took charge of the Tate Creek Development Company.

ASSETS

Land contracts owing by settlers to T.C.D.C.........	$47,392.10	
Less $250.00 allowable Dec. 1, 1943	$26,750.00	$20,642.10
Unassigned land — 5,567 acres—including 363 acres cultivated (Value based on 1939 price......		$ 7,060.00
34 Unassigned buildings (Valued by Mr. H.B. Sommerfeld)		$ 3,580.00
Power and other machinery (Valued by CCA Supervisors)......................		$ 5,070.00
Repair parts and tools (Valued by CCA Supervisors)..		$ 588.65
Seed Grain, tractor fuel, lumber (Valued by CCA Supervisors)......................		$ 636.93
Lumber camp buildings, equipment and ties (Valued by CCA Supervisors)......................		$ 967.00
Office and household equipment (Valued by CCA Supervisors)......................		$ 338.40
Feed grain — sold to Tate Creek Co-op Society		$ 851.68
1941 Wheat acreage Reduction Bonus for grasses		$ 368.00
Balance of Settlers' advance accounts		$ 163.70
Balance of Blacksmith's Equipment account		$ 416.75
Total Assets...............		$40,683.21
Total Liabilities of the T.C.D.C. as at the end of 1942 was a balance owing on land purchase contracts in the amount of:.................................		$10,258.15
Net Balance:............		$30,425.06

Source: Sudeten Settlement in Tomslake A Progress Report by the Canada Colonization Association July, 1955.

LAND AND IMPROVEMENTS

	Total Acreage	1942 Cultivated Acreage	Land & Improvements Assigned at Cost	1955 Cultivated Acreage	Land & Improvements Estimated Present Value.
A. Lands assigned by TCDC to 107 settlers in 1942	18,107	2,782	$49,904.00	6,631	$255,536.00
B. Land purchased from TCDC since 1942 by 25 settlers	3,790	(At Purchase) 355	(Pursh. Price) 9,185.00	511	13,735.00
C. Lands purchased from other than TCDC—since 1942 by 12 settlers	3,504	203	14,450.00	882	17,819.00
C. Dwellings including wiring and lots owned by settlers residing in the hamlet of Tomslake					10,870.00
Totals	25,401	3,340	$73,539.00	8,024	$297,960.00

Source: *Sudeten Settlement in Tomslake. A Progress Report by the Canada Colonization Association, July, 1955.*

BUILDINGS AND OTHER IMPROVEMENTS

Buildings and other improvements individually owned by settlers are summarized as follows: —

Kind	1942 Number	1942 Value	1955 Number	1955 Value
Dwellings	115	$17,250	98	$55,220
Barns	95	12,350	105	20,315
Milk Houses	—	—	31	1,870
Hog Houses	89	5,150	49	4,630
Hen Houses	92	2,000	56	2,655
Garages	—	—	38	2,755
Granaries	89	5,000	266	16,650
Sheds	36	1,100	50	2,785
Barbed wire fencing	50 miles	2,000	224 miles	11,200
Wells	12	1,500	8	1,700
Dugouts and Dams	10	500	57	2,850
Creeks and Rivers	32	3,000	32	3,200
Electric Wiring	—	—	64	17,620
Dwellings including wiring and lots owned by individual settlers residing in Tomslake	—	—	6	10,870
Total of all buildings and improvements individually owned		$49,850		$154,320
Buildings including wiring and lots owned collectively i.e. Co-op. Store, Community Halls, etc.			4	25,350
Buildings owned by T.C.D.C.	34	3,580	4	303
Total of all buildings and improvements in Settlement (not including schools and churches).		$53,430		$179,973

Source: Sudeten Settlement in Tomslake. A Progress Report by the Canada Colonization Association July, 1955.

LIVESTOCK INVENTORY

Kind	1942		1955	
	Number	Value	Number	Value
Horses	209	$10,450.00	123	$ 6,150.00
Milk Cows	—	—	341	42,625.00
Other Cows	263	13,150.00	83	8,300.00
1 and 2 year olds	'307	7,000.00	(234	17,550.00
Calves			(241	6,025.00
Bulls	9	700.00	19	2,850.00
Sows	143	2,860.00	41	1,640.00
Hogs	1,193	11,930.00	385	7,700.00
Sheep	—	—	36	540.00
Poultry	3,227	1,600.00	2,084	2,084.00
TOTALS		$47,690.00		$95,464.00

Source: Sudeten Settlement in Tomslake. A Progress Report by the Canada Colonization Association July, 1955.

EQUIPMENT AND MACHINERY INVENTORY

	1942		1955	
Automobiles	1	$ 800	9	$ 13,250
Trucks (mostly ½ or ¾ ton)	2	1,500	18	25,770
Tractors	1	700	65	110,645
Combines	—	—	5	9,650
Swathers	—	—	1	800
Grain separators	—	—	8	8,160
Binders	20	2,500	64	14,360
Mowers	32	1,600	62	5,505
Rakes (5 of these are side delivery)	17	800	57	4,045
Plows (52 of these are tractor plows)	38	1,900	80	15,670
Breaker Plows — brush	—	—	8	735
One-way discs	1	250	21	6,570
Double discs	—	—	20	3,055
Single discs	33	1,400	31	1,065
Drag harrow sections	120	600	268	2,125
Cultivators	—	—	5	755
Grain Drills	24	3,000	59	13,973
Packers	—	—	6	395
Wagons (23 of these are rubber tired)	50	3,000	115	9,555
Sleighs	40	1,800	81	3,040
Hay balers	—	—	7	7,425
Crushers or Hammermills (4 are H. Mills)	2	200	38	3,841
Posthole diggers	—	—	4	330
Feed cutters	—	—	4	230
Fanning mills	—	—	4	290
Circular saws	3	100	43	1,330
Weed sprayers	—	—	2	220
Cream separators	60	2,700	55	2,130
Milking machines	—	—	10	1,800
Water pumps	2	100	17	974
Stationary gas engines	—	—	7	350
Electric motors	—	—	9	541
Saw mills	—	—	4	2,100
Miscellaneous (2 road scrapers, 1 fertilizer attachment, 1 blacksmith outfit)	1	500		1,060
TOTALS		$23,450		$271,744

Source: Sudeten Settlement in Tomslake. A Progress Report by the Canada Colonization Association July, 1955.

SETTLEMENT ASSETS, LIABILITIES AND NET WORTH

Assets	1942	1955
Land and buildings—in farms	$ 49,904	$287,090
Land and buildings—in Tomslake	—	10,870
Machinery	23,450	271,144
Livestock	47,690	96,214
Cash and receivables	2,000	16,428
TOTALS	$123,044	$681,746
Liabilities		
On Land	$20,652	$20,900
Buildings		1,005
Machinery		32,043
To Bank		13,690
Private debts		2,490
TOTALS	$ 20,652	$ 70,128
SETTLERS NET WORTH—Estimated:	$102,392	$611,618

To this "net worth" should be added the net assets of:
The collectively owned buildings such as the Co-op Store
    and Community Halls. $ 25,350
The T.C.D.C. Land, Buildings and Machinery.
    (The T.C.D.C. has some other assets not included here) $ 13,246
TOTAL NET WORTH OF SETTLEMENT—Estimated: $650,214

Sources: Sudeten Settlement in Tomslake. A Progress Report by the Canada Colonization Association July, 1955.

FARM EARNINGS AND OUTSIDE EARNINGS

Source	1942 Amount	1954 Amount
Sale of whole milk	$ —	$ 60,251
Sale of cream	4,300	3,072
Sale of hogs	32,300	14,224
Sale of cattle	5,570	23,551
Sale of poultry and eggs	100	969
Sale of grain	—	14,695*
Sale of clover seed and hay	—	914
Outside earnings by settler	20,000	96,677
Outside earnings by settlers' dependents		12,280
TOTAL INCOME	$62,270	$226,633

*Some of this grain was sold to settlers within the settlement for feed and seed.

The average gross income for 1954 of the 21 inactive owner-operators was $1,535.00.

The average gross income of the 10 owners who rent their lands to others was $2,136.00.

The average gross income of the 66 active owner-operators was $2,622.00.

LAND USE and CROPPING PATTERN in 1954:

The following table shows the use made by settlers during 1954 of their cultivated lands:

	1942*			1954		
	Total Acreage	Yield	% of Total Cultiv'd.	Total Acreage	Yield	% of Total Cultiv'd.
Wheat	184	4,161	5.8	57	596	.7
Oats	1,130	49,761	36.0	2,816	56,658	35.1
Barley	756	23,451	24.0	1,113	14,537	14.1
Green Feed	227		7.2	265		3.3
Summerfallow	308		9.8	1,145		14.3
Tame Grass Hay	160		5.1	1,562		19.5
Tame Grass Pasture				430		5.3
Clover Hay				527		6.6
Clover Pasture				33		.2
New Breaking	380		12.1	70		.9
Total Cultivated	3,145	77,373	100	8,018	71,791	100
Uncultivated Woods and Pasture	14,962			17,383		
Total Acreage	18,107			25,401		

*Includes T.C.D.C. operated lands.
Source: Sudeten Settlement in Tomslake. A Progress Report by the Canada Colonization Association July, 1955

LAND USE AND CROPPING PATTERN (CONTINUED)

Grain crop yields in the settlement since 1941 have been as follows: —

Year	Wheat		Oats		Barley		Total	
	Acres	Bushels	Acres	Bushels	Acres	Bushels	Acres	Bushels
1942	184	4,161	1,130	49,761	756	23,451	2,070	77,373
1943	123	3,120	1,255	48,098	912	30,025	2,290	81,243
1944	138	2,161	1,322	37,186	1,078	19,099	2,539	58,446
1945	123	1,895	1,609	49,081	957	20,231	2,690	71,207
1946	155	5,615	1,921	117,217	757	26,427	2,833	149,259
1947	127	1,592	2,174	66,089	837	7,975	3,138	75,656
1948	96	1,427	2,475	79,727	578	11,778	3,149	92,932
1949	430	7,791	3,300	122,826	640	13,836	4,370	144,453
1950	438	2,651	3,020	39,410	530	3,822	3,988	45,883
1951	350	7,000	2,400	98,000	650	20,000	3,400	125,000
1952	No report							
1953	No report							
1954	57	596	2,816	56,658	1,113	14,537	3,986	71,791
Av. yield per acre		17			33		22	

Source: Sudeten Settlement in Tomslake. A Progress Report by the Canada Colonization Association July, 1955.

ASSETS AND LIABILITIES OF THE TATE CREEK DEVELOPMENT COMPANY

The following inventories for the years 1939, 1942 and 1954 indicate the financial position of the company at these periods:

ASSETS

	1939	1942	1954
Land contracts owning by settlers		$20,642.10	$ 470.02*
Unassigned land — acres		5,567.00	1,600.00
Unassigned land — value		7,060.00	1,090.00
Unassigned buildings — No.		(34)	(4)
Unassigned buildings — value		3,580.00	303.38
Power Machinery		5,070.00	10,710.55
Seed grain, tractor fuel, lumber		636.93	—
Lumber camp buildings, equipment, ties		967.00	4.86
Office and household equipment		388.40	257.17
Feed grain		851.68	—
1941 wheat acreage Reduction Bonus		368.00	—
Balance of settlers advance accounts		163.70	—
Balance of blacksmith's equipment account		416.75	—
Victory loans		—	600.00
109 shares Tomslake Community Centre		—	1,090.00
Accounts receivable from settlers-work	—	4,348.10*	
Accounts receivable inventory sales		—	3,075.26*
Cash in Bank or on Hand	$260,000.00	$3,600.00	275.80
	$260,000.00	$44,333.21	$23,105.36

LIABILITIES

Balance of Land Purchase Contracts		$10,258.15	
Loans			4,548.11
TOTAL NET ASSETS	$260,000.00	$34,075.06	$18,557.25

*These figures taken from 1953 report.

Source: *Sudeten Settlement in Tomslake. A Progress Report* by the Canada Colonization Association July, 1955.

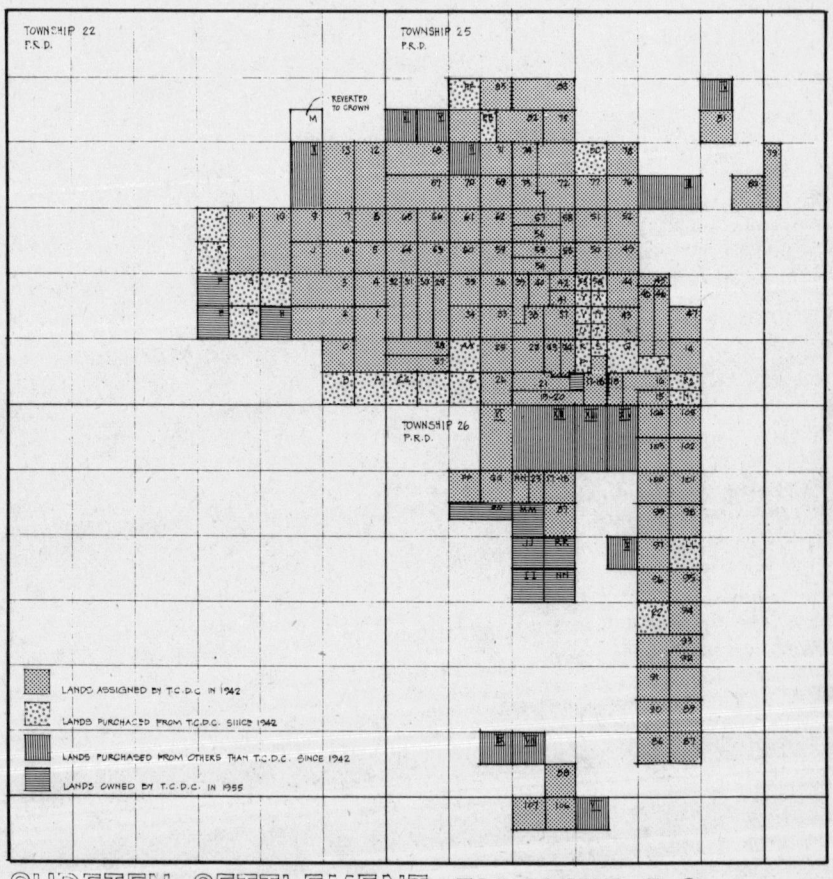

SUDETEN SETTLEMENT · TOMSLAKE B·C·
land distribution diagram · july 1955

APPENDIX II

Male Settlers at Tupper Creek, 1939

Amstatter, Andrew (8)
Andersch, Afthur (29)
Arbter, F.
+ Augsten, Anton
+ Aust, J.
Axmann, Robert
Barth, Josef (11)
+ Bartel, Berthold
Bartusek, Ernst (3)
+ Baudisch, Johann (38)
Bauernfeind, Robert
+ Brenner, Willi
Burdak, Karl (41)
Brumlik, Arnold (53)
Cepa, Alfred
+ David, Alfred (71)
+ Dill, Johann (12)
Dill, Erhard (7)
Dietl, Willi (30)
+ Dittrich, Valentin (18)
+ Dittrich, Karl (34)
Dostal, Hermann (101)
Dotzauer, Roman
Dworsky, Rudolf
Eckert, Hubert (104)
Eckert, Erwin
Erhard, Frank
Englisch, Paul (36)
Englisch, Fritz
Englisch, Hans
Etzler, Rudolf
+ Fischer, Alois (42)
+ Fister, Karl, Sen. (14)
Foster, Willi
+ Frank, Heinrich (92)
Gabriel, Frank (86)
Gebhard, Frank (20)
Gebhard, Richard (19)
+ Dr. Glas, Arnold (24)
+ Goldbach, Ernst (81)
+ Grundl, Alfred
Hampl, Richard (4)
+ Haeckl, William (10)
Hanke, Fritz sen. (82)
+ Harles, Norbert (23)

+ Hegenbarth, Frank (97)
Hein, Ehrich
Heyne, F.
Heinrich, Josef (66)
Heller, Herbert (102)
+ Herold, Adolf (45)
Hilbert, Alois (58)
+ Hillebrand, Fritz (64)
Hirsch, Max (44)
Hirschman, Hermann
Hocke, Rudolf
Hoidn, Rudolf (78)
Hopp, Alois
+ Jellinek, Karl
+ Jilg, Ewald (27)
Klimpl, Wenzel
Koblischek, Frank
Koecher, Josef (80)
Kolenz, J.
+ Konrad, Josef
+ Krassa Fritz (48)
Kraus, Rudolf
+ Korbay, Alois (83)
Koutnik, Ernst
Kopp, Anton (70)
Krotil, Karl
Kreuzinger, Josef (16)
Kreuzinger, Walter
Kreuzer, Ernst (40)
Kuttig, Frank (100)
Kuempfl, Reinhold
+ Kuenzel, Frank (15)
Kutschker, Alois (69)
+ Klemmer, Frank (46)
+ Landsfried, Rudolf (84)
Langer, Adolf
+ Langer, E. (99)
Langhammer, Frank
+ Leinsmer, Hubert (56)
Lexa, Herbert
Liney, Josef (106)
+ Lorenz, Ed
+ Loeffler, Frank

Lutz, Willi
Mader, Rudolf
Mann, Otto
Mahrhofer, Frank (72)
+ Marek, Karl
+ Mayer, Hugo
+ Mazanek, Henry (37)
Mollik, Alois (37)
+ Mueller, Frank (95)
+ Mueller, Alois
+ Neubauer, Konrad (75)
Neubauer, Anton (85)
+ Nettek, Josef (76)
+ Nodes, Josef (88)
+ Oesterreich, August
+ Pickert, Ernst (5)
Papouschek, Rudolf (59)
+ Poellman, F.
Poppe, Alois (68)
+ Priegert, Gottfried (67)
Prezcek, Bill
Rabas, Anton
Rei, Alfred
Reilich, Frank
+ Reinelt, Fridolin (49)
Richter, Leo
Richter, Frank (63)
+ Riedel, Florian (25)
+ Ritschel, Karl
+ Roth, Wenzel (89)
Salinger, Emil
Sedlacek, W.,
+ Seidel, Karl I. (52)
Seidel, Hermann (51)
Seidel, Karl II. (94)
+ Seitner, Alois (103)
+ Siegert, Max Otto (43)
+ Singer, Karl
+ Snehota, Frank (28)
+ Sommert, Nicu (107)
+ Suttner, Frank
+ Schaffer, Ed.
+ Scharing, Julius sen.
Scharnagl, Fred
Scherbaum, Georg (91)
+ Schindler, Ivo (74)
+ Schindler, Anton (93)
Schlosser, Eduard
Schneider, Walter (79)

Schneider, August (73)
Schneider, Frank (31)
+ Scholz, Alois (1)
Scholz, Ferdinand
+ Schoen, Willi (61)
Schoenpflug, H.
+ Schoeder, Frank (6)
+ Schoenstein, Karl (32)
Schroefel, Rudolf
Schroefel, Oskar
Schwarz, Dr. Harald (65)
Schwertner, Willi (105)
Sternschein, Prof.
+ Stoehr, Albert
Stoehr, Eric
Stoehr, Adolf
Stoehr, Josef
+ Steinl, Walter
Tamm, Frank (54)
+ Tillner, Josef (57)
+ Tschiedel, Rudolf (98)
Ullmann, Josef
Vogel, Albert
+ Vodermeyer, Ed.
Voit, Rudolf (26)
Wagner, Karl H.
Wagner, Hans
Wagner, Alois
+ Wagner, Karl II.
+ Wagner, Johann sen. (87)
Wagner, Ed.
Waller, Georg (55)
Wanka, Willi (13)
+ Wanka, Frank (9)
Watzl, Anton (96)
+ Wedrich, Frank (47)
Weider, Josef
Weniger, Georg
+ Weigel, Ernst (50)
+ Weinhart, Josef (21
Weisbach Henry
Wattengel, Ernst
Wetzler, Konrad
Wiesner, Herbert (62)
+ Winter, Josef (22)
+ Wolfinger, Frank (17)
+ Woerl, Ignatz
+ Woerl, Michael

+ Wurst, Rudolf
+ Zapf, Frank (77)
+ Zamburek, Leo
+ Zieglarsch, Johann (90)

NOTE: *All the names marked + are now deceased. The numbers in brackets behind the names correspond with numbers on the land map and show the location of the 107 settlers, who actually were settled in 1942. The remaining prospective settlers in this list moved away to other locations—mainly in Eastern Canada.*

NOTES ON SOURCES

Sources used to develop the outline of the historical roots of the Sudeten German people and their relations with the Czechs are as follows:

Czechs & Germans: A Study of the Struggle in the Historic Provinces of Bohemia and Moravia. Elizabeth Wiskeman. Second Edition. St. Martin's Press. New York. 1967.
Europe's Road to Potsdam. Wenzel Jaksch. Translated and edited by Kurt Glaser. Thames and Hudson. London. 1963.
The Sudeten Problem 1933-1938. Ronald M. Smelser. Wesleyan University Press. Middleton, Connecticut. 1977.
The Vanguard of the "Drang Nach Osten". Vojta Benes. Czechoslovak National Council of America. Chicago. 1943.
The Transfer of the Sudeten Germans: A Study of Czech-German Relations 1933-1962. Radomir Luza. New York University Press. 1964.

Sources for the discussion of the Canada Colonization Association is from the Canadian Pacific Papers, Glenbow Alberta Institute Library and Archives, Calgary, Alberta. Other sources for the material presented are as acknowledged in the text and appendices or from the **Medicine Hat News,** Medicine Hat, Alberta.

Suggestions for Further Reading

European History
The Struggle for Mastery in Europe 1848-1915. A.J.P. Taylor. Oxford University Press. London. Reprint 1974.
The Origins of the First World War. H.W. Koch, editor. The Mac-

The Long Fuse: An Interpretation of the Origins of World War I. Laurence Lafore. Second edition. J.B. Lippincott Company. Philadelphia. 1971.

A History of Germany 1815-1945. William Carr. Edward Arnold (Publishers) Ltd. London. Reprint 1974.

Europe 1914-1939. F. Lee Benns and Mary Elizabeth Seldon. Prentice-Hall Inc. Englewood Cliffs, N.J. 1965.

Documents on Nazism, 1919-1945. Introduced and edited by Jeremy Noakes and Geoffrey Pridham. The Viking Press. New York. 1974.

The Nazi Years. A Documentary History. Edited by Joachim Remak. Prentice-Hall Inc. Englewood Cliffs, New Jersey. 1969.

Nazi Culture. Intellectual, Cultural and Social Life in the Third Reich. Edited by George Mose. Grosset & Dunlop. New York. 1966. The Universal Library Edition 1968.

They Thought They Were Free. The Germans 1933-45. Milton Mayer. The University of Chicago Press. Chicago. 1955.

The End of Glory. An Interpretation of the Origins of World War II. Laurence Lafore. J.B. Lippincot Company. 1970.

Diplomatic Prelude. 1938-39. L.B. Namier. MacMillan & Co. Ltd. London. 1948.

Germany's Eastern Neighbours: Problems Related to the Oder-Neisse Line and the Czech Frontier Regions. Elizabeth Wiskemann. Oxford University Press. London. 1956.

The History of the Czechoslovak Republic. 1919-1948. Victor S. Mamatey and Radomir Luza, editors. Princeton University Press. 1973.

I Saw the Crucifiction. Sydney Morrell. Peter Davis Ltd. London. 1939.

Fallen Bastions: The Central European Tragedy. G.E.R. Gedye. Victor Gollancz Ltd. London. 1939.

Czechoslovakia Enslaved: The Story of the Communist Coup d'Etat. Hubert Ripka. Victor Gollancz Ltd. London. 1950.

The German Catastrophe. Reflections and Recollections. Friedrich Meinecke. Translated by Sidney B. Fay. Beacon Press. Boston. 1963.

The Victors and the Vanquished. Heda Kovaly and Erazim Kohak. Horizon Press. New York. 1973.

Lost Fatherland: The Story of the Mennonite Emigration from Soviet Russia, 1921-1927. John B. Toews. Herald Press. Scoltdale, Pennsylvania. 1967.

Canadian History
Canada: Immigration and Colonization 1840-1903. Norman MacDonald. Macmillan of Canada. Toronto. 1970.
Only Farmers Need Apply. Harold M. Troper. Griffin House. Toronto. 1972.
A Short History of Western Canada. J.W. Grant MacEwan. McGraw-Hill Ryerson Ltd. Toronto. 1968.
The Opening of the Canadian West. Douglas Hill. A Windjammer Book. Longman Canada Limited. Don Mills, Ontario. 1973.
Homesteader: A Prairie Boyhood Recalled. James M. Minifie. Macmillan of Canada. Toronto. 1972.
The Great Crash of 1929. John Kenneth Galbraith. Second edition. Houghton Mifflin Company. Boston. 1961.
Men Against the Desert. James H. Gray. Western Producer. Prairie Books. Saskatoon. 1967.
The Winter Years. James H. Gray. The Macmillan Company of Canada. Toronto. 1966.
Ten Lost Years, 1929-1939. Barry Broadfoot. Paperjacks. Don Mills, Ontario. 1973.
Land of the Second Chance. A History of Ethnic Groups in Southern Alberta. Howard Palmer. The Lethbridge Herald. Lethbridge, Alberta. 1972.
Next Year Country. Jean Burnet. University of Toronto Press. Toronto. 1951.
Esterhazy and Early Hungarian Immigration of Canada. Martin Kovacs. Canadian Plans Studies. Regina. 1974.
Wappella Farm Settlement. (The First Successful Jewish Farm Settlement in Canada). Historical and Scientific Society of Manitoba and Jewish Historical Society of Western Canada. Winnipeg. 1971.
Ethnic Groups in British Columbia. British Columbia Centennial Committee. 1967.
The Enemy that Never Was. A History of the Japanese Canadians. Ken Adachi. McClelland and Stewart. 1976.
Western Canada's Enemy Aliens in World War One. Joseph A. Bourdreau. Alberta Historical Review. Vol. 12. 1964.
The Czechs and Slovaks in Canada. John Gellner and John Smerek. University of Toronto Press. Toronto. 1968.
Men in Sheepskin Coats. Vera Lysenko. Ryerson Press. Toronto. 1947.
Vilni Zemli (Free Lands). **The Ukrainian Settlement of Alberta.** J.G. MacGregor. McClelland and Stewart. Toronto. 1969.
Thirty Years: Sudeten Emigration 1938-68. Dawson Creek. Published privately. 1968.

PRINTED IN CANADA